faith

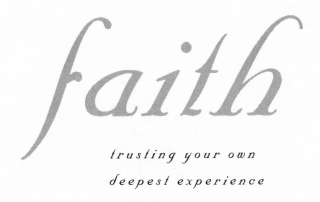

faith

trusting your own

deepest experience

SHARON SALZBERG

RIVERHEAD BOOKS

A MEMBER OF

PENGUIN PUTNAM INC.

NEW YORK 2002

From *Lalla: Naked Song,* translated and copyright © Coleman Barks, reprinted by permission of the translator.

From "East Coker" in *Four Quartets,* copyright 1942 by T. S. Eliot and renewed 1970 by Esme Valerie Eliot, reprinted by permission of Harcourt, Inc.

From "East Coker" in *Four Quartets,* copyright by T. S. Eliot, reprinted by permission of the publishers, Faber and Faber Ltd.

From "Autumn" by Rainer Maria Rilke, translated and copyright © Jonathan Cott, reprinted by permission of the translator.

RIVERHEAD BOOKS
a member of
Penguin Putnam Inc.
375 Hudson Street
New York, NY 10014

Library of Congress Cataloging-in-Publication Data

Salzberg, Sharon.
Faith : trusting your own deepest experience / Sharon Salzberg.
p.   cm.
ISBN 1-57322-228-3
1. Salzberg, Sharon.   2. Buddhists—United States—Biography.
3. Spiritual biography.   4. Faith (Buddhism).   I. Title.
BQ984.L7A3   2002   2002017901
294.3'092—dc21
[B]

Printed in the United States of America
1   3   5   7   9   10   8   6   4   2

This book is printed on acid-free paper. ∞

Book design by Marysarah Quinn

*To my teachers,
who have taught me how to live,
and why.*

acknowledgments

So many people have helped me since 1996, when the idea first came to me to write a book about faith, that I couldn't possibly name them all. Among them are wonderful friends who have helped shape my understanding of faith through discussion, inspiration, or the example of their lives. They include Joseph Goldstein, Tara Bennett-Goleman, Dan Goleman, Sarah Doering, Ram Dass, Sunanda Markus, Mark Epstein, Bob Thurman, Lila Anderson, Maggie Spiegel, Dorothy Austin, and Sylvia Boorstein.

Several wise and generous people either helped guide me through the publishing process, gave me feedback on the manuscript, or reminded me that the essence of good writing is to "tell the truth," and pointed out when I fell short of that. They include Amy Gross, Mark Matousek, Tracy Cochran, Naomi Wolf, Patty Gift, Elizabeth Cutthrell,

Marsha Norman, Dean Ornish, Jonathan Cott, Barbara Graham, Kate Wheeler, Catherine Ingram, and Jeff Zaleski.

In the course of writing this book I have been sheltered, fed, supported, and befriended by Ann Buck, Jen Greenfield, Gina Thompson, Daidie Donnelly, Julie Tato, Anne Millikin, Fred Hanson, the staff, board, and teachers of IMS, Davine Fox, Mitch Kapor, and my extraordinary yoga teacher John Friend. Gyano Gibson and Eric McCord, the home team, provided the essential platform that kept the rest of my life going so that I could write. Eric did everything from help me find the missing toolbar on the computer on a Saturday morning, to permissions, to all levels of computer support. Gyano helped me make numerous difficult choices about what needed to be said, entered changes for what seemed like a million hours in LA, and has steadfastly accompanied me throughout the many byways of this journey.

Shoshana Alexander first sat down with me in 1997, to ask what I would want to say in a book about faith. Since then she has interviewed me to help discern what I really did want to say, helped create a structure when there was none apparent, helped create a new structure whenever I changed my mind, taught me about writing, and edited at least ten drafts of most chapters. Joan Oliver did many hours of research, gave me much moral support, and added immeasurably to the manuscript through her refined sense of language and precision of expression. Cathy Saypol, in a burst of intuition, gave me a subtitle.

I owe a great debt to my agent, Joy Harris, who was once described accurately to me as "the closest you'll ever come to unconditional love in a business relationship." Her caring and clarity have held me through this whole process, from the time I first appeared in her office saying, "I'm not really a writer, I'm a meditation teacher," until this moment.

Without Amy Hertz, my editor at Riverhead, this book would never have come into being. Amy has always trusted me, even when I've been discouraged or confused, and her clear vision, remarkable intelligence, and professional standards have sustained the whole project and brought my work to an entirely different level.

Special thanks to Krishna Das, whose CDs kept me company many times at 2 A.M. as I was writing, and whose chanting always brings me back to the things I care about more than anything; and to the people I've taught and meditated with in NYC, who through the years have become good friends, and who, since September 11, have kept reminding me of what faith looks like.

contents

INTRODUCTION xiii

CHAPTER 1

the journey of faith 1

CHAPTER 2

falling in love: bright faith 24

CHAPTER 3

verifying faith:
claiming the right to question 44

CHAPTER 4

faith and fear 74

CHAPTER 5

despair: the loss of faith   98

CHAPTER 6

faith in action   124

CHAPTER 7

abiding faith: faith in ourselves   150

EPILOGUE 174

introduction

ONE DAY A FRIEND called to ask if we could meet for tea. Knowing that I was writing a book on faith from the Buddhist perspective, she was confused and wanted to talk. "How can you possibly be writing a book on faith without focusing on God?" she demanded. "Isn't that the whole point?" Her concern spoke to the common understanding we have of faith—that it is synonymous with religious adherence. But the tendency to equate faith with doctrine, and then argue about terminology and concepts, distracts us from what faith is actually about. In my understanding, whether faith is connected to a deity or not, its essence lies in trusting ourselves to discover the deepest truths on which we can rely.

For some this will be a very different approach to faith. Many link faith to narrow-minded belief systems, lack of intelligent examination, or pain at having one's questions silenced. Faith might evoke images of submission to an external authority. Historically, the idea of faith has been used to slice cleanly between those who belong to a select group and those who do not. To fuel their own embittered agendas, fanatics harness what they call faith to hatred.

I want to invite a new use of the word faith, one that is not associated with a dogmatic religious interpretation or divisiveness. I want to encourage delight in the word, to help reclaim faith as fresh, vibrant, intelligent, and liberating. This is a faith that emphasizes a foundation of love and respect for ourselves. It is a faith that uncovers our connection to others, rather than designating anyone as separate and apart.

Faith does not require a belief system, and is not necessarily connected to a deity or God, though it doesn't deny one. This faith is not a commodity we either have or don't have—it is an inner quality that unfolds as we learn to trust our own deepest experience.

The Buddha said, "Faith is the beginning of all good things." No matter what we encounter in life, it is faith that enables us to try again, to trust again, to love again. Even in times of immense suffering, it is faith that enables us to relate to the present moment in such a way that we can go on, we can move forward, instead of becoming lost in resignation or despair. Faith links our present-day experience, whether wonderful or terrible, to the underlying pulse of life itself.

A capacity for this type of faith is inherent in every human being. We might not recognize it or know how to nurture it, but we can learn to do both. This book is the story of my own journey of faith. May it serve to support and enhance your own.

the journey of faith

EACH OF US tells ourselves some kind of story about who we are and what our life is about. Our theme might be the pursuit of money, sex, or prestige; it might center on love or spirituality. Some of us figure as a hero in the story, some as an antihero. Our story might be picaresque, romantic, or tragic. We might frame ourselves as optimists or pessimists, winners or losers. How we interpret our own experiences gives rise to the narratives to which we dedicate our lives. Some stories weave the fragments of our experience into a greater whole, in a way that reveals relationship and connection. Other stories lock us into the fragments, leaving us nowhere to turn.

As is the case for many, the story I told myself for years was that I didn't deserve to be happy. Throughout my childhood, I believed that something must be intrinsically wrong with me because things never seemed to change for the better. My father, whom I adored, disappeared when I was four, and my mother and I moved in with my aunt and uncle. One night when I was nine years old, my mother and I were home alone. She had recently undergone surgery and seemed to be recovering well. In celebration of her return, I was wearing my ballerina Halloween costume. We were sitting close together on the couch, watching her favorite singer, Nat King Cole, on television, when suddenly she began bleeding violently. I ran out into the hallway to get someone to help us, but couldn't find anyone. My mother managed to tell me to call an ambulance immediately and then to call my grandmother, whom I hardly knew, to come get me. Shaking uncontrollably, I complied. After that evening, I never saw her again. About two weeks later she died in the hospital. After that, I lived with my father's parents and rarely heard mention of my mother again.

My childhood continued to unfold through terrifying, uprooting turns and incomprehensible losses. When I was eleven my grandfather died, and one day my father returned. The handsome prince I'd secretly imagined had been replaced by a disheveled, hard-bitten, troubled stranger. A few days after he arrived, my entire body broke out in hives. When I got back from the doctor's office, my father told me, "You have to be tough to be able to survive life." Six weeks later he took an overdose of sleeping pills. I stood outside in the cold, holding my grandmother's hand among a crowd of gawking neighbors as he was carried out on a stretcher. I watched as the flashing red lights receded and the sirens faded. Now both of my parents had been spun away from me in the back of an ambulance. That night my father entered the mental health system. He was never able to function outside of it again.

One of the hardest parts of all the loss and dislocation was that it was surrounded by an ambient, opaque silence about what was happening. Because no one spoke openly or even acknowledged all the changes as loss, my immense grief, anger, and confusion remained held inside. Whenever the cover slipped, I scrambled to hide the feelings, or distort them, so no one would really know, especially not myself. When John Kennedy was assassinated, I couldn't stop crying. My grandmother asked me why, and I replied, simply, "Because his children have lost their father."

The story I was telling myself was that what I felt didn't matter anyway. It seems as if I spent most of my childhood, and even my teenage years, curled up in bed, lost in a separate shadowed existence built of sadness. I repeatedly invented scenarios of having parents just like anybody else. The dream of answering, just like anybody else, the schoolteacher's question, "What does your father do for a living?"

was the kindling that fed the fire of many of my secret fantasies. I'd summon images of my mother coming back, as though from a long trip, like anyone else's mother might. But I wasn't at all like anybody else seemed to be. Of course, none of them were like they seemed either, but I didn't know that then. Feeling so different, I liked playing it safe more than anything, seeing life from a distance, never really engaging, preferring to lose myself in the seductive play of listlessness.

While silent dreams and desires played out within me, in most situations I'd insist with bravado, "I didn't want that anyway." When I lived with my grandparents, color television was just becoming the rage. I longed for one, but they couldn't afford it. To compensate, my grandmother, who cared a lot about me, bought a special plastic sheet to place over the black-and-white screen to create a faint illusion of color. This rainbow aura bore no relationship to the figures and settings of the stories depicted in the programs. I wanted to rip off that bizarre front and plead for the real thing; instead I silently tolerated the charade, not betraying my desire. I didn't care about anything, or so I hoped it seemed. I came to know very well the protection of distance, of a narrowed, compressed world. Though it was my own act of pulling back, I felt forsaken. I told myself a story that there was no way out of the world that turned me in upon myself.

. . .

YEARS LATER, as an adult, I would find the phrase that perfectly described my dilemma. Some friends and I had rented a house near the ocean where we could practice meditation on our own for a few days. In my designated bedroom I found a "Peanuts" comic strip on the desk, which went something like this: Lucy is sitting in a little booth, a DOCTOR IS IN sign prominently displayed. She tells Charlie Brown, "You know what your problem is, Charlie Brown? The problem with you is that you're you." Crushed, Charlie Brown asks, "Well, what in the world can I do about that?" Lucy responds in the final frame, "I don't pretend to be able to give advice. I merely point out the problem."

"The problem with you is that you're you" was a very familiar phrase—the "me that was me" was someone I had often considered a problem. Many of us seem to have an internalized Lucy, who tells us that our problem is who we are and that there is no way out, little reason to have faith in ourselves or in the possibility of turning our lives around.

In fact, until I was eighteen, Lucy ruled. My resistance to participating more fully in life came to feel like the most alive, vibrant thing about me. I often found myself, in many endeavors, not really trying because I was secretly sure that I'd fail. I'd learned well to hold life in abeyance. For years, I hardly spoke. I barely allowed myself a full-blown emotion—no anger, no joy. My whole life was an effort to balance on the edge of what felt like an eroding cliff where I was stranded. I was waiting, suspended. Though it mimics death, waiting isn't necessarily death's prelude, but might rather be the life-force conserving itself. When I was a child my favorite animal was a caterpillar, never a dog or a cat, and somehow never a butterfly. Like the body being cooled down before surgery to slow its vital functions, my very life depended on stepping out of time and expectation, depended on waiting for . . . *something.*

At sixteen I entered the State University of New York at Buffalo, feeling as lost and afraid as ever. By this time the smooth, monochromatic shelter of abeyance, which had once saved me, was now engulfing me. I was slowly being forced to wake up out of my slumber. Having to choose an academic major confronted me with defining what I wanted out of life. Just that one choice provoked the uncertainty and risk of discovering what it might mean to be alive. Sometimes I thought of majoring in history, sometimes in philosophy. I heard that the Asian studies department offered a philosophy class on Buddhism, and I enrolled.

ONE OF THE BUDDHA'S basic teachings is that because we are born, we experience suffering—not only suffering as grave pain, but also suffering as the instability, the sorrow, the hollowness of life. Sometimes the distress is simply dissatisfaction that things don't go the way we wish they would. Sometimes the discomfort is minor; sometimes the pain is unspeakable. When I heard this First Noble Truth, I knew it to be true. The circumstances of my own life proclaimed it.

The Second Noble Truth talks about the causes of suffering as ignorance and attachment. I wasn't too sure what attachment meant, but figured I might understand by the end of the semester. The teaching about ignorance of who we are was intriguing. The Second Noble Truth says that we look at our personal histories, our bodies, our thoughts and feelings, and we conclude, "That's who I am." But when we look to these things to know who we actually are, we become consumed and exhausted. Within ten minutes we might see sadness, amusement, anger, kindness; we might feel physical pleasure, then discomfort, then relief, then apprehension as the discomfort emerges again. We might see ourselves as powerful one moment, powerless the next. As our thoughts and feelings and sensations shift and change, any superficial idea of who we are unravels. We may strive mightily to hold it together, because we fear being nothing, being nowhere. As long as we are ignorant of what lies below our surface identifications, the teachings say we will be unhappy.

Is there a way out? The Third Noble Truth affirms that

without reservation. This Truth is described in different ways: as wisdom that understands fully the nature of life; as liberation from distorted concepts of who we think we are by seeing clearly who we actually are; as boundless, unimpeded love for ourselves and all others without exception; as experience of that which lies beyond our conditioning, that which frees us from suffering.

The meditation techniques developed by the sages of old, embedded in the Fourth Noble Truth, were said to be the way to achieve this liberation. All of this suggested a radically different way to tell a life story—the way the Buddha told it. In commenting on the power of a story to give our lives cohesion, writer Hannah Arendt says, "The story reveals the meaning of what otherwise would remain an unbearable sequence of sheer happenings." To perceive the events of our lives as "sheer happenings" is indeed unbearable. I was about to explore a story that would take the scattered shards of my life and fit them all together in a new and different way.

The Buddha's story is about freedom from suffering. It is a way out of Charlie Brown's problem. A way to trust our immense potential, instead of that belittling Lucy voice. I was captivated by the possibility of turning my life around, of lifting it out of the resignation and sorrow that had been the background notes of my own personal story. Some inner knowing of what I had been waiting for was stirred.

. . .

THE PIVOTAL POINT of the Buddha's story is his enlightenment. Siddhartha Gautama, born an Indian prince,
was a *bodhisattva:* he aspired to become a buddha, an awakened one, so that he could help relieve all beings of suffering. After years of trying various methods to purify his
mind and attain understanding, he sat down under a tree
one night, determined not to move until he was free of all
confusion, all ignorance, and all limitation. While he sat
deep in meditation, he was attacked by the legendary figure
Mara—killer of virtue, killer of life. With enticing and lust-
ful visions, with ferocious rain and hailstorms, with vile
images, Mara attempted to dissuade him from his course.
But, through it all, Siddhartha sat tranquilly.

It is significant that Mara's ultimate attack was on the
bodhisattva's faith in his own potential. In essence Mara
said, "Who do you think you are to be sitting there with
that immense aspiration? What makes you think you can
actually be enlightened?" This was Lucy in the voice of
Mara. In response to that challenge, the bodhisattva reached
his hand down and touched the earth, asking it to bear witness to all the lifetimes in which he had practiced generosity and morality, lovingkindness and wisdom. He asked the
earth to bear witness to his right to be sitting there, his
right to aspire to full understanding and infinite compas-

sion. As the legend goes, when the bodhisattva touched the ground, the earth shook, testifying to his right to be free. With that, Mara was vanquished and fled. The bodhisattva sat through the rest of the night in deep meditation, and with the rising of the first morning star was enlightened.

In this story is the Buddha's promise that freeing the mind from habits of anguish and fear is a real and attainable goal, not just for him, not just for a few others, but for everyone who makes the effort. That all beings want to be happy, and in fact deserve to be happy, is emblazoned throughout.

Our ingrained habit of viewing life as though standing with our noses pressed against the bakery window, believing that none of the goodies inside could possibly be for us, runs right up against this boundless, breathtaking inclusivity. The voice of the inner Lucy puts us outside that bakery window, saying, "Life, freedom, happiness, love are for others, not for you." The Buddha holds out his hand, offering to bring us directly inside. Here was a promise that I could finally live unencumbered by the pain of my past. This view of what life could be drew me like a magnet.

In my second year of college, although my life was slowly opening up, the only time I really came alive was for an hour and a half on Tuesdays and Thursdays, in my Asian philosophy class. I found myself beginning to wonder if I might one day be truly happy, even though my family didn't look at all like anything I'd dreamed it should be. Maybe I didn't have to be lonely and afraid forever. Maybe I didn't have to be so pressed down by my circumstances forever. While the repeated disintegration of my family had kept me frightened, this glimmer of possibility kept me alive.

Like a subliminal message being played under the predominant music, a sense of possibility, no matter how faint, drives a wedge between the suffering we may wake up with each day and the hopelessness that can try to move in with us on a permanent basis. It inspires us to envision a better life for ourselves. It is this glimmer of possibility that is the beginning of faith.

When I learned about the school's junior-year-abroad program, I felt strongly attracted. Despite the fact that the only time in my life I had even left New York State was for a short trip to Florida, I felt ready to leave everything I had known and travel to a place about which I knew nothing. I could no longer simply endure, could no longer be half-alive and willing merely to get by. I yearned for embodiment, for a sense of belonging; I yearned to transform the waiting into finally coming alive. I wanted to take up my place in the world.

When I tell people I decided to go to India when I was only eighteen, they often think I knew what I was doing.

Once someone remarked, "You must have been such a clear thinker," and I had to reply, in all honesty, "No, in fact I only had one clear thought," which was that I could solve the "problem" that was me if I learned how to meditate. That one clear thought was enough. It would set me on a journey that would remake my life.

IN PALI, the language of the original Buddhist texts, the word usually translated as faith, confidence, or trust is *saddha*. Saddha literally means "to place the heart upon." To have faith is to offer one's heart or give over one's heart. The "unbearable sequence of sheer happenings" that had been my life began to come together in the teachings of the Buddha, and I was ready to place my heart upon those teachings. Perhaps I already had. The promise of happiness had touched a place within me so deep and unknown that what it had awakened there was wild, inchoate, primal. I recognize that now as the stirring of faith.

In Pali, faith is a verb, an action, as it is also in Latin and Hebrew. Faith is not a singular state that we either have or don't have, but is something that we do. We "faithe." Saddha is the willingness to take the next step, to see the unknown as an adventure, to launch a journey. Writer and philosopher John O'Donohue holds up the story of Aeneas, hero of Virgil's epic poem about the founding of Rome, as an archetypal journey of faith. When Aeneas flees the battle of Troy, he has no idea of where he is going or what lies before him. On his way to do one thing, he finds himself, blown by storm and fortune, doing another. His ships and crew are battered, plundered, attacked, but, guided by a faint yet compelling sense of mission, Aeneas again and again faces the unknown. Only when he has the courage to step into the darkness, as O'Donohue depicts it, does the light to guide him to the next step reveal itself.

Often it is the journey itself, not the destination, that is the real point of setting forth. For me, the journey from the isolation of my early life to the doorway of freedom has been the unfolding of my faith, because I had to be willing, like Aeneas, to keep moving forward, even when I felt I was walking in the dark. With faith we move into the unknown, openly meeting whatever the next moment brings. Faith is what gets us out of bed, gets us on an airplane to an unknown land, opens us to the possibility that our lives can be different. Though we may repeatedly stumble, afraid to move forward in the dark, we have the strength to take that magnitude of risk because of faith.

The first step on the journey of faith is to recognize that everything is moving onward to something else, inside us and outside. Seeing this truth is the foundation of faith. Life is transition, movement, and growth. However solid things may appear on the surface, everything in life is changing,

without exception. Even Mount Everest—the perfect symbol of indomitable, unyielding, massively solid reality—is
"growing" a quarter of an inch a year, as the landmass of
India pushes under Asia. People come and go in our lives;
possessions break or change; governments and whole systems of government are established or disintegrate. Eager
anticipation precedes a meal, which soon ends. A relationship is difficult and disappointing, then transforms into a
bond we trust. We might feel frightened in the morning,
reassured in the afternoon, and uneasy at night. We know
that at the end of our lives we die. There is change, breath,
oscillation, and rhythm everywhere.

With faith we can draw near to the truth of the present
moment, which is dissolving into the unknown even as we
meet it. We open up to what is happening right now in all
its mutability and evanescence. A pain in our body, a heartache, an unjust treatment may seem inert, impermeable,
unchanging. It may appear to be all that is, all that ever will
be. But when we look closely, instead of solidity, we see
porousness, fluidity, motion. We begin to see gaps between
the moments of suffering. We see the small changes that are
happening all the time in the texture, the intensity, the con-
tours of our pain.

No matter what is happening, whenever we see the inevitability of change, the ordinary, or even oppressive, facts

FAITH

of our lives can become alive with prospect. We see that a self-image we've been holding doesn't need to define us forever, the next step is not the last step, what life was is not what it is now, and certainly not what it might yet be.

Some years ago, when I was teaching meditation at a federal women's prison in California, one of the inmates observed, "When you're in prison, it's especially important to try to live in the present moment. It's easy to get lost in the past, which you can't change anyway, or to get lost hoping for the future, which is not yet here. If you do that, it's like you're not really alive." Then she paused and looked at me, her eyes shining, and said, "I choose life."

Such faith is not superficial or sentimental. It doesn't say everything will turn out all right. As we all know, as I knew profoundly by the time I was eighteen, a lot of times things don't turn out "all right," according to our wishes, according to our demands or ideas of how they should. Life is not likely to deliver only pleasant events. Faith entails the understanding that we don't know how things will unfold. Even so, faith allows us to claim the possibility that we ourselves might change in ways that will allow us to recognize and trust the helping hands stretched toward us. It enables us to aspire to a better life than the one we have inherited.

Without faith in change we would be compelled to repeat patterns of suffering—like an abused child who grows up to find an abusive partner—at least reassured by being able to predict mortification and pain. Without a sense of possibility, we would be stuck—isolated, hopeless, and unspeakably sad.

Faith is the animation of the heart that says, "I choose life, I align myself with the potential inherent in life, I give myself over to that potential." This spark of faith is ignited the moment we think, *I'm going to go for it. I'm going to try.*

I once asked a psychiatrist friend what he considered the single most compelling force for healing in the psychotherapeutic relationship. "Love," he replied. I agreed with him about the transforming power of love but wondered if there wasn't something else even more fundamental. "For all we know," I suggested, "what is most important to healing in therapy is that people show up for their appointments." The therapist's love can nurture healing, but it is our own faith in that possibility that impels us to show up and take each new step into the darkness.

To seize such possibility for myself, I first had to reach within the lassitude coiled tightly around my heart and begin transforming how I felt about my heart and about myself. I had to give up my protective distance, alter my habit of withdrawal, and learn to participate, engage, link up. I had to acknowledge that underneath my facade of indifference, I cared, and in fact cared a lot. I cared about what happened to me and what happened to others. I cared about life.

I stepped onto the spiritual path moved by an inner sense that I might find greatness of heart, that I might find profound belonging, that I might find a hidden source of love and compassion. Like a homing instinct for freedom, my intuitive sense that this was possible was the faint, flickering, yet undeniable expression of faith.

THE BREAKOUT MOMENT of faith was my decision to travel to India without knowing where to go once I got there. A few days before my departure, Chogyam Trungpa Rinpoche, a Tibetan Buddhist teacher, was scheduled to speak in Buffalo. I decided to go. Trungpa Rinpoche was the first practicing Buddhist I'd encountered. His background seemed very exotic. After completing his religious studies, then serving as abbot of a group of monasteries in eastern Tibet, Trungpa Rinpoche led a party of three hundred refugees in a dramatic escape to India to flee Chinese oppression. Later he left India for Oxford, England, where he studied Western philosophy. This was his first trip to the United States.

Instead of mysterious robes, Trungpa Rinpoche was dressed in a business suit. He wasn't ethereal at all, but had a solid-looking body, with a pronounced limp. A gently amused look played around his eyes. Though he was warm toward the audience, the impression he gave was that he was saying what he simply felt to be true—it wouldn't have mattered if two people were listening, or two thousand, or if we were all slyly doing our homework instead of listening at all. I found Trungpa Rinpoche's presence magnetic, but almost frightening; he seemed still, very still, under his eloquent delivery—not the girded stillness of restraint, or of prudence, but of something I'd never witnessed before. It was an alive stillness, as if his words were emerging from a place of quiet deep within him. If there was a similar place of quiet deep within me, I'd certainly never been there.

After his talk, Trungpa Rinpoche asked people to submit written questions. Mine happened to be the first piece of paper he picked out of the huge stack in front of him. Trungpa Rinpoche read the question aloud: "In a few days I am leaving for India to study Buddhism. Do you have any recommendations as to where I should go?" He was silent for a few moments, then in his precise British accent he replied, "In this matter you had perhaps best follow the pretense of accident." That was it—no names or addresses, no maps, no directions.

What could he mean by "the pretense of accident"? This was the first intimation that I might be embarking on a journey unlike anything I could imagine or predict.

. . .

I ARRIVED at the New Delhi train station, having traveled overland from Europe through Afghanistan and Pakistan. The moment I stepped off the train I was assaulted by the intensity of India. Insistent young men surrounded me, demanding to carry my bags. Vendors pushed close and loudly hawked their wares. Gaunt women carrying infants came over to me, begging for money, as did old men with broken bodies. I saw a *sadhu* for the first time, a half-naked mendicant smeared with ashes to signify the inevitability of death. All around him children chased one another, laughing loudly. Throngs of people and animals pressed in on me. I had never seen life displayed so openly before, had never felt it pulsing so fiercely, with joy and suffering all jumbled together. Nothing seemed hidden, and there was nowhere for me to hide. In the sultry air, diesel fumes, antiseptic, and dust mingled with layers of jasmine and frangipani. Standing in the midst of it, even though it was so new, so intense, I was glad I'd come.

A few days later I traveled north by train and then jeep to Dharamsala, home of the Dalai Lama and a great portion of the Tibetan Buddhist refugee community. Dharamsala is poised on a spur of the snowcapped Dhauladhar Mountains, the foothills of the Himalayas, which surround the town on three sides as a breathtaking backdrop. Dense pine forests cover the hillsides, and masses of rhododendrons grow alongside the paths. Playful monkeys scamper over the rooftops. The Tibetan culture is maintained here by way of crafts and traditional arts and dances, as well as a medical institute that teaches the ancient and revered Tibetan system of healing, a children's village for refugees and orphans, and the monasteries that preserve the Tibetan Buddhist teachings and practices. I was immediately captivated by the Tibetan people, who had lost almost everything, yet survived in exile largely because of their spiritual faith.

Over the next couple of months I attended various classes taught by Tibetans I had heard about from other Westerners. I began to realize that the tradition prevalent there emphasized study of religious texts before beginning meditation practice. Though I loved what I did learn of the teachings, I grew impatient to learn meditation, to see if it would give me what I was looking for.

To my relief, I finally heard about a teacher who offered practical meditation instruction. The following morning I walked along the mountain trails to the scheduled class only to find that it had been canceled because the teacher was sick. The next time I went, the teacher had recovered but the translator was away, so once again the class was called off. Frustrated, I waited a week for the next class, trudging up the trail only to find that both teacher and translator had gone off on a trip of unknown length. I began to wonder if I'd ever get any meditation instruction at all. It was growing harder to trust life enough to live by the "pretense of accident"—to trust that opportunities were always there.

Then one day, while sitting in a local restaurant, I overheard an American woman casually mention an international yoga conference about to take place in New Delhi. Thinking that I might find a meditation teacher there, I left Dharamsala and made my way back to New Delhi. At the conference, I encountered swamis and yogis galore, but no one I felt drawn to accept as a teacher.

That old familiar sinking feeling started to return. For months I had been grappling with how to find someone to teach me meditation while also trying to find something I could safely eat, remembering to look for cows before crossing the street, avoiding the monkeys who would bite when intentionally or unintentionally provoked, and figuring out how to live with only what I could carry. I was beginning to wear down.

One day the conference hit a low point when several of the presenters started shoving each other to grab the microphone and be the first to speak. I felt horribly dispirited. I had come all the way to India to find a holy person. Now I wondered if that was even possible.

I thought of leaving New Delhi, but I didn't know where to turn in intense, tumultuous India. I was sorely tempted to withdraw, to declare that searching for a guide was stupid and futile, and that I didn't care at all anyway. But each morning I found myself getting up and returning to the yoga conference, not sure of what I'd find, but spurred on by a flickering faith that just wouldn't let me give up.

On the final day of the conference, I heard a paper read by Daniel Goleman, an American who decades later wrote the best-seller *Emotional Intelligence*. At that time he was a graduate student in psychology, doing research in India. At the end of his talk he mentioned a Buddhist meditation retreat he was about to attend in Bodhgaya, along with Ram Dass, a spiritual leader I had heard speak back in Buffalo. I had found Ram Dass's lecture there inspiring, and I was eager to meet him. Immediately I decided to join the group formed of several people who had attended the talk, and go with them to Bodhgaya.

My new story was about to begin. It would be one that explores what happens when, in the face of any circumstance, whether joyful or painful, we choose to have faith in generosity, kindness, and clear seeing. It would be the story of learning to have faith in our own innate goodness and capacity to love. It would be the story of seeing past the apparent randomness of "sheer happenings" to uncover layers and layers of connection. It would be the story of knowing, even in the midst of great suffering, that we can still belong to life, that we're not cast out and alone. This new story was the Buddha's story. I would work to make it my own.

falling in love: bright faith

I ARRIVED IN BODHGAYA in late December 1970 and fell in love. I fell in love with the meditation teachers I found there, and with the community of students who gathered around them. I fell in love with the Buddha's teachings. I fell in love with the place. Even discomfort and uncertainty didn't tarnish the romance. Getting to Bodhgaya involved a seventeen-hour ride from New Delhi in a train so crowded that people were hanging out the windows. This was followed by a wild hour in a bicycle rickshaw with the driver pedaling furiously to outrun any lurking bandits.

Arriving so late meant that finding a place to sleep would be difficult. Finally my companions from the New Delhi yoga conference and I were allowed to put our sleeping bags down on the dining room floor of a tourist hotel. I woke to roosters crowing, dogs barking, women chatting at the water pump outside, and prayers being broadcast over loudspeakers. Blaring Hindi film music drowned out everything else. It was the dawning of a hot, dry, dusty day, and the beginning of my new life.

I stepped out into the golden light of Bodhgaya. Warm and pervasive, it wrapped itself around the vibrant colors of roadside spice stands, the curling smoke of charcoal and wood blazes, the rainbow-hued women's saris, the saffron, and the ocher and burgundy robes of Buddhist monks and nuns. In that glow, boundaries blurred and softened.

The half-mile walk to the center of town from my hotel presented an array of new sights. I passed a Thai pagoda and a Chinese temple; teams of water buffalo plowed the patchwork of rice fields between them. At the edge of the marketplace there was a Tibetan restaurant, housed in a large, dingy tent, and surrounded by tea stalls made of wooden boards tacked together at odd angles. Peanut vendors, roasting nuts on hot ashes, called out the excellence of their product, and old men proffered huge baskets of tiny bananas, deep lavender eggplants, bright green chilis, oranges, and pomegranates. A blind beggar held out his hand for alms, and scrawny dogs hunted for scraps of food. A couple of cars made their way through this scene, honking incessantly, and two men prodded an elephant down the road. I fell in love with this teeming wonder of life.

Just past the market is the center of Bodhgaya, and the center of the Buddhist universe—the bodhi tree under which the Buddha sat while he achieved enlightenment. A direct descendant of the original tree grows at the same spot now, a highly venerated shrine.

Covered with shiny, dark green heart-shaped leaves, the bodhi tree rises majestically, its arms spread wide, as if holding the sky. In Buddhist legend, it is said that after his enlightenment the Buddha stood for a full week gazing in gratitude at the tree that had sheltered him. Now I was beholding the tree, absorbing the feel of it, yearning for the protection of its immense arms. My heart leaped. For the first time in my life, I understood the sacredness of a place, how it could possess a transporting power and open the door to a new way of looking at the world. Tibetan Buddhists had strung prayer flags between the bodhi tree's lower branches, so that the wind could carry prayers for all beings around the entire globe. As I watched them flapping, I realized that perhaps as a child I had been less alone than I had thought.

Next to the bodhi tree stands the Mahabodhi temple, commemorating the wondrous freedom of mind the Buddha attained there. Gathered around it were devotees ringing bells in ancient ritualized rhythms, pilgrims burning incense, and clusters of monks and nuns whispering prayers or singing them aloud in a cacophony of languages. A young man in saffron robes was being ordained into monastic life, and dozens of Tibetan practitioners performed full-length prostrations to convey their respect to the Buddha and to purify their minds.

Despite all the mantras and prayers, movement and activity, I experienced a profound quiet. It was as though an echo of the Buddha's awakening, 2,500 years earlier, still lingered in the air. Centuries of people honoring the place and what it represented about human possibility had only added to the calm. I felt the stillness as a force field, penetrating my own jumbled mind, widening and enlarging the space within until my thoughts were less like hammers striking an anvil and more like ripples on a quiet sea. My body and mind felt at peace with the world.

As I circled the bodhi tree, I came upon a ragged elderly man in the burgundy robes of a Tibetan monastic. His lips moved silently in prayer as he counted the beads of his *mala,* similar to a rosary. He looked up at me, smiled, and offered me a seed from the bodhi tree, motioning to me to eat it. I popped it into my mouth, not stopping to think of any symbolic significance to his gesture, or of the transfiguration we might have just celebrated. Then the monk indicated that I should sit next to him. I later found out that this simple, kind, and unassuming man was a renowned scholar and practitioner, Khunu Rinpoche, whose many students included the Dalai Lama.

Khunu Rinpoche served as my welcoming committee
to a world different from any I had known, a world that offered release from the dominion of suffering. In my Buddhism class at college I had read about the Third Noble
Truth—liberation from suffering—but didn't yet know
how that might apply to the intensity of my own pain. Here
I recognized the possibility in the feeling of the air, in the
kindness of Khunu Rinpoche's eyes, in the murmurs of
Buddhist texts being recited out loud, in the compassion
symbolized by the prayer flags. They were the promise of
the Third Noble Truth come alive.

As I sat next to Khunu Rinpoche, I sensed deep within
me the possibility of rising above the circumstances of my
childhood, of defining myself by something other than my
family's painful struggles and its hardened tone of defeat. I
recalled the resignation in my father's eyes at the constraints
that governed his life. The boundary of his autonomy was
the decision about where to have lunch if someone took
him out of the hospital on a pass. With a surge of conviction, I thought, *But I am* here, *and I can learn to be truly free.*
I felt as if nothing and no one could take away the joy of that
prospect.

This state of love-filled delight in possibilities and eager
joy at the prospect of actualizing them is known in Buddhism
as bright faith. Bright faith goes beyond merely claiming
that possibility for oneself to immersing oneself in it. With

bright faith we feel exalted as we are lifted out of our normal sense of insignificance, thrilled as we no longer feel lost and alone. The enthusiasm, energy, and courage we need in order to leave the safe path, to stop aligning ourselves with the familiar or the convenient, arises with bright faith. It enables us to step out, step away, and see what we can make of our lives. With bright faith we act on our potential to transform our suffering and live in a different way.

We might be so touched by the mystery or sacredness of a place, as I was by the bodhi tree, that we are filled with bright faith. Or it might arise when we meet or hear of someone who moves us profoundly. My friend Sunanda recalls meeting her teacher, Neem Karoli Baba, at his ashram in India. Her immediate impression was that he seemed to somehow fill the room with love. Something inside her sighed deeply, as if this feeling of pervasive love was what she had been missing her whole life, and she was only now complete.

Sunanda stayed in India another six months. For the first three, whenever she saw Neem Karoli Baba she was so moved she'd burst into tears. Her strong sense of devotion to him made her determined to take to heart his core teaching, "Love everybody, serve everybody, always remember God." She vowed to try to live by that maxim for the rest of her life.

Sometimes we read something inspiring and feel so filled

with bright faith that we break out of our normal routines and challenge previously cherished assumptions. When my friend Denise read *The Flight of the Eagle* by J. Krishnamurti, she was astonished to find put into words what she felt was in her blood. Denise didn't know whether Krishnamurti was still alive, but by calling the number noted in the back of the book, she found out about a lecture series he'd soon be giving in England. At once she called a travel agent. When Denise entered the tent where Krishnamurti was teaching, she felt an incredible, almost palpable beauty. The promise of bright faith had led her to a context that was deeply fulfilling; she stayed, working at his school, for more than four years.

Bright faith can resemble blind faith: Both tend to be inspired by something or someone outside ourselves that can send us off on sudden journeys around the world in pursuit of a dream. But blind faith has a pejorative connotation: It is associated with an unthinking devotion to a teacher or teaching that is mistakenly seen as the fulfillment of the journey of faith rather than an early step. Bright faith can have the same dangers as blind faith. However, in Buddhism, bright faith is seen simply as a beginning, and not a beginning in which we surrender discriminating intelligence, but rather one in which we surrender cynicism and apathy. Its abundant energy propels us forward into the unknown.

. . .

THE RETREAT I'd come to attend took place on the grounds of the Burmese temple on the outskirts of town, overlooking the river where, legend has it, Siddhartha Gautama broke his fast to strengthen his body before his final sojourn to Buddhahood under the bodhi tree. About a hundred Westerners were gathered there within the temple complex, its high gate making it a wholly separate enclave, a world unto itself.

Our teacher was an Indian man named S. N. Goenka, a former businessman first drawn to meditation as a means to cure his ferocious migraine headaches. Goenka had studied Buddhism in Burma, then a few months before I arrived in Bodhgaya had begun leading ten-day intensives in which participants lived like monastics, taking only two meals a day and following a highly structured schedule of meditation practice and instruction. Each evening students would learn something of the Buddha's teaching through lectures and small discussion groups.

Outwardly, Goenka resembled an ordinary Indian businessman. But he radiated something extraordinary from within. Centered, unruffled, he seemed completely comfortable in his own skin. Goenka was rigorous in his approach to teaching meditation: precise in his instructions and demanding the very best effort from his students. Yet his kindness and compassion charged the air around him with warmth and light. In a classic display of bright faith, I was enthralled. I wanted more than anything to edge closer to that warmth. Goenka seemed deeply dedicated to helping his students achieve happiness. My faith blazed brighter in his inspiring presence.

Most of us gathered there were inexperienced in meditation. The anticipation of beginning a unique adventure together was in the air. Goenka laughed a lot, spoke to us in simple English, and was quite approachable. He explained that it was traditional to begin a retreat by taking refuge in the three jewels: the Buddha, the *dharma,* and the *sangha.* We were about to open ourselves, he told us, to a deep process of seeing—and freeing ourselves from—old patterns, and we would need to feel a sense of safety in order to accomplish this.

All of us go through times in our lives when we feel as if we are lost in a wilderness, caught in a violent storm. Exposed and vulnerable, we look for something or someone to help us through the upheaval. We look for a place of safety that won't break apart no matter what we are experiencing. As many of us have discovered, the refuge we may have sought—in relationships, in ideals, in points of view—ultimately lets us down. We begin to wonder, *Is there any refuge that is real and enduring?* On that first evening of the retreat, Goenka offered assurance that the answer to that question could be yes.

Finding a spiritual refuge is a significant step on the journey of faith. A trustworthy refuge enables us to go against the misleading promises of an unexamined world, to move beyond conditioned attitudes and responses, to eschew superficial or heartless answers to our deepest questions.

Goenka seemed to be speaking directly to me, his words catapulting through the space between us, landing in the center of my heart. I had been yearning for a refuge, a safe home. I could see that my fleeting thoughts and feelings were no more a safe haven than the continuously shifting, often wrenching experiences of my life had been. I needed a refuge wholly different from anything I already knew.

Goenka led us in the traditional formula for taking refuge, by reciting the following phrases three times in Pali, then having us repeat them back: *Buddhaṁ saranaṁ gacchāmi* (I take refuge in the Buddha); *dhammaṁ saranaṁ gacchāmi* (I take refuge in the dhamma, or dharma as it is commonly known from the Sanskrit); *sanghaṁ saranaṁ gacchāmi* (I take refuge in the sangha). I spoke the words with my whole heart. Over my many years of involvement with the Buddhist tradition, I have heard people demur at using foreign words in the refuge recitation. Some have asked not to do it in Pali, or even in translation, because it makes them uncomfortable. That is perfectly understandable. But for myself, I love taking refuge. I love the ceremonial feeling of it, the deliberate acknowledgment of the forces of wisdom in the world. I love opening myself to an expanded view of what my own life could be like. I love the ritual of looking for the best within myself. Most of all, I love the sense of celebration, of joining with others all the way back to the Buddha in an adventure of freedom.

The first refuge, the Buddha, refers to begin with to the historical person Siddhartha Gautama, the man who once ate a meal across the road from the Burmese temple and then got enlightened a few blocks away. While he is variously depicted as a mystic, a legendary figure, a historical teacher, and a leader, he is portrayed foremost as a human being, with human capacities. He asked the kinds of questions any of us might ask about the nature of our existence: What does it mean to be born in a human body, vulnerable and helpless, then to grow old, get sick and die, whether we like it or not? What does it mean to have a human mind that can careen through anger, joy, lust, pride in the space of a morning? Is there a quality of freedom and happiness that won't disappear as the conditions of our lives change? What can we trust? The Buddha can be an inspiration because he set out to answer those questions and succeeded. It is taught that the Buddha discovered the answers not through revelation from a supreme being, but through the power of awareness that is inherent in all of us. For some, he is a refuge by virtue of this inspiration. For devotional Buddhists, he is a refuge because they perceive him as a living energy, capable of providing loving shelter.

On that first evening of the retreat, however, Goenka took care to explain that taking refuge in the Buddha doesn't require calling yourself a Buddhist or adopting any dogma or feeling devotion to a particular being. Whether or not we have any interest in Buddhism as a religion, the potential to realize the Buddha's insight, compassion, and courage is a part of who we already are. The word "buddha" means one who has completely awakened from ignorance, one who has fulfilled his or her vast potential for wisdom and compassion. A buddha resides in each of us as the potential for the awakened mind. Each one of us has the capacity to fully understand our lives, and to be free.

We can look at the Buddha and see ourselves, we see all that we can be. We can look at ourselves and we see not just one person's potential, but the capacity for freedom, the nascent buddha within everyone. Taking refuge in the Buddha was, for me, like having an uncommon mirror held up before me, and seeing myself in ways I hadn't before—rich with the potential for transformation, and possessed of innate beauty. Hearing my own inner world portrayed as containing such seeds of abundance filled me with joy. I felt it was safe to go forward in this new exploration.

The second refuge is the dharma. The word "dharma" in Sanskrit has several interrelated meanings. In the broadest sense, dharma means the truth, the laws of nature, the way things are: Deciduous trees lose their leaves in winter; change occurs despite our efforts to stop it; unwelcome thoughts arise unbidden in our minds no matter what we will; if I tell lies my mind will be filled with fear and uncertainty.

The more clearly we see the dharma, the way things are, the more clearly we see the inevitability of impermanence, the natural flow of joy and sorrow, the possibility of freeing our minds from entangling thoughts and finding happiness that won't vanish as our minds and bodies change. Like being close enough to the ocean to hear the rhythm of the surf underneath ordinary conversation, being in touch with the dharma means hearing underlying truths pulse throughout the ordinary events of our lives. As poet Rainer Maria Rilke observed, "Don't be confused by surfaces; in the depths everything becomes law."

Dharma also means the Buddha's teachings, such as the Four Noble Truths: suffering, the cause of suffering, the end of suffering, and the way to the end of suffering, which is the path of morality, concentration, and insight. When I studied them in college, the Four Noble Truths had been a mere concept; here in Bodhgaya they were being described as a way of life, a practical set of tools to make our lives dif-

FAITH

ferent. Taking refuge in the dharma, we are taking refuge in
a vision of life that extends beyond our usual, limited sense
of who we are and what we are capable of.

The third refuge is the sangha, the community of those
who, throughout history, have sought freedom from suffering and have come to a real and personal awareness of that
freedom. Listening to Goenka, I could almost feel the presence of the women and men who, for centuries, had the
faith to walk a spiritual path, to set forth into the unknown,
to challenge habit and let go of the convenient and familiar in order to find an end to suffering. Each one had personal conditioning to untangle, lives to understand, loss
and fear with which to wrestle, and hearts to offer. If they
could awaken to the truth of life, Goenka was telling us, we
also could.

As the vision of sangha seeped into my mind, I realized
that by honoring the inspiration of others who had walked
this path before me I was also discovering a new sense of
my own heritage. Alongside generations of Polish Jewish
peasants who were my ancestors, I could see all the women
and men who had followed the dharma in their own ways,
discovering the same truths that I was being invited to uncover. Never before had I so fully recognized my intimate
connection to those who had lived before me. For a moment, time collapsed and we were all together—my bio-

logical ancestors who had brought me to that point and the spiritual ancestors who were urging me onward.

And the sangha wasn't just out there somewhere in history, I realized. It was all around me. Goenka and Khunu Rinpoche seemed as loving and benevolent as any depiction of the Buddha I'd seen. I began to understand that those who are committed to realizing the truth can animate potential within us that might otherwise lie dormant. This urgency within them to be truthful, to wake up, not to waste their lives can light a sense of urgency in us as well. The fire within them lights a fire within us. In the light of that flame, I felt a shelter of love and connection. Taking refuge in the sangha, I could feel the force of life itself, without beginning or end, cascading through me, and I fell in love with the thrill of at last belonging to a greater whole.

I shyly looked around the room. Coming from the United States, Canada, South America, Europe, and Australia as well as India, we had gathered there together. I didn't know it then, but several of those sitting there would become my closest friends—Joseph Goldstein and Ram Dass among them. All of us were taking refuge together. These one hundred people had had faith enough to take this meditation course. They had made a courageous commitment to understanding themselves, and I felt somehow joined to their faith and courage by taking refuge with them. Together we had been following a call.

. . .

THE BUDDHA once told this story about faith: A herd
of cows arrives at the bank of a wide stream. The mature
ones see the stream and simply wade across it. The Buddha
likened them to fully enlightened beings who have crossed
the stream of ignorance and suffering. The younger cows,
less mature in their wisdom, stumble apprehensively on the
shore, but eventually they go forward and cross the stream.
Last come the calves, trembling with fear, some just learning how to stand. But these vulnerable, tender calves also
get to the other side, the Buddha said. They cross the stream
just by following the lowing of their mothers. The calves
trust their mothers and, anticipating the safety of reunion,
follow their voices and cross the stream. That, the Buddha
said, is the power of faith to call us forward.

In Bodhgaya, at my first meditation retreat, I was like a
newborn calf in my bright faith, and the Buddha's voice,
full of love, promised to lead me home. The voice of the
dharma was showing me how to get there, step by step. The
voice of the sangha was reminding me that I wasn't traveling alone.

It had been nine years since my mother died. As we recited the three refuges together, I could hear the voice of
the archetypal mother beckoning—wise, watching out for
me, welcoming, caring, always present. I offered my heart

in response. Vibrating with energy and inspiration, I felt a sense of promise and hope I'd never felt before.

BY THE END of my first full day of practice, I wondered if I was insane to be there. I was in tremendous physical pain. My back ached and my knees were on fire from trying to sit for so many hours in the classic cross-legged meditation posture. Added to the discomfort of an unfamiliar position was the deeply held tension in my body, just starting to reveal itself. I was a bundle of knots. I had been so excited to learn meditation. This was it?

The first few days, Goenka instructed us to focus our attention on the in and out breath at the nostrils, then later, on the sensations experienced throughout our bodies. The technique was easy to understand but not so easy to accomplish. Even harder to bear than the physical pain was the long-buried sorrow and anger that were beginning to emerge. I was unsettled. What had I thought meditation would be? If this was liberation from suffering, something must be wrong.

Outside the scheduled meditation sessions, I sat in the courtyard, in the shade of a large mango tree, trying to follow my breath. During meals, sitting on the dining hall floor eating curries off banana-leaf plates, I tried to follow my breath. Goenka had told us, "Continuity of practice is the secret of success." Though I could barely remember at times what that success might be, I kept trying. I wanted nothing more than for my mind to center on a still point, to focus on the moment, to feel a flow of subtle sensation through my body. Most of the time my attention wandered all over the place. And my body was either numb or blasting with pain.

Despite how badly I felt, every evening I would listen to Goenka's discourse and fall in love all over again with the Buddha's teaching. My bright faith spurred me on to face another miserable day of practice. Then one day, something happened. I sensed a startling shift inside. At times the pain lifted and I felt a lightness and clarity that reminded me of the glimpse of freedom I'd experienced standing under the bodhi tree. I was beginning to see something entirely new about myself.

Whatever remaining doubts I had about being in the right place were dispelled on the final day of the retreat. Goenka introduced another traditional meditation practice—*metta,* or lovingkindness. Metta, he explained, is a practice of friendship. We were to fill our bodies and minds with the energy of kindness and love, and then, starting with ourselves, to offer this goodwill to an ever-widening circle, until it included all beings everywhere. As waves of warmth and love passed through my body and mind, my bright faith burnished to a fiercer glow. I had never felt so at home, never been so happy.

. . .

LATER THAT DAY, I walked through the temple gates and down the road into town to sit once again under the bodhi tree. I found it, as always, in the midst of a swirl of activity yet bathed in the mystery of a lustrous silence. I felt so happy to be there, linked a little more closely now to the beneficence that had arisen 2,500 years earlier in that spot. The texts say the Buddha spent his final night under the tree in deep concentration, attending to his breath, the power of his focus rending the last veils of ignorance. Now as I sat there following my own breath, calming my mind, I could hear the omnipresent prayer flags flapping in the wind, extending boundless compassion to all beings.

I reflected back on the ten-day retreat and on all that I had learned. I remembered the fleeting moments of concentration and how peaceful they had been. I remembered the depth and beauty of the lovingkindness meditation. All that inspired me, with the vitality of bright faith, to become the best person I could possibly be.

There under the bodhi tree, I asked myself what I most wanted this inner journey to yield. The answer welled up from my heart: "I'm practicing so that I can have the love of a buddha, so I can love other people the way the Buddha did." That morning, I fell fully in love with a new vision of what my life might look like. I felt ablaze with a glorious sense of possibility and aspiration.

The Buddha said that he was born "for the good of the many, for the welfare of the many, out of compassion for the world." He was born, then, for me, and for all beings, to offer a path to freedom. I had taken the first baby steps on that path.

To continue on my journey of faith, I would need to deepen my understanding. I would need to learn how to channel the erratic, brilliant fire of bright faith into a steady, illuminating glow. Beyond the first intensity of love and encouragement that is bright faith, we must arrive at an inner faith not dependent on externals, something we can carry with us, that isn't born only of the compelling mirror held up by another, or the resonant vibrations of a sacred place, or a wonderful feeling of possibility. We need a faith based on our own experience, reached with eyes wide open. Undertaking this task would force me to challenge, to lose, and ultimately to deepen my faith.

verifying faith:
claiming the right
to question

BRIGHT FAITH, with its exhilarating sense of discovery, makes for a wonderful beginning to a spiritual journey. But it can make for a faltering middle if it's all we have to count on, and for a bad end if we are unwilling to go deeper. Bright faith is necessary but not sufficient. Eventually that blaze of glorious feeling must be grounded and refined through some very hard work.

Intoxicated by the vision of possibility laid before us by bright faith, we can shallowly chase one dream after another, forgetting the steadfast effort needed to make any dream come true. Unless we translate our inspiration into the effort to actualize our dreams, our faith will remain immature. Floating in its delight, each day we can be swayed by any new influence in front of us, believing without question whatever is offered.

In my own case, I had a strong tendency to place my faith in authority figures, in teachers I found fascinating and admirable, rather than working to develop faith in my own strengths through practice. Soon after my first retreats with Goenka, who was so exacting and precise, I fell in love with two other remarkable teachers. Munindra, an Indian teacher who had spent many years in Burma, was living in Bodhgaya. Whimsical and elfin, he dressed all in white and strongly resembled Gandhi. His relaxed way of teaching could be summed up in one of his favorite sayings, "Just be simple and easy about things." Demanding long hours of structured, disciplined meditation practice was not his style. Instead, he taught that every action in our lives can be meditation. One of the favorite stories that circulated among his students was of a time several of them were wandering through the marketplace of Bodhgaya with him. As they watched Munindra bargain, first with the peanut vendor, then with the cloth merchant, one student questioned whether bargaining like that was appropriate for a spiritual teacher. Munindra replied, "The practice of the dharma is to learn to be simple, not to be a simpleton."

Munindra was so unassuming that children spontaneously gathered around him in the streets, especially when he stopped to rejoice at the sight of a tree or a flower or a pig. As I watched Munindra, all thoughts of clarity and precision vanished. I wanted to be as free and easy as he was,

to marvel at the tiniest flower, to be surrounded by enraptured children.

When I met Dipa-Ma, who had been a student of
Munindra's, I saw her as the epitome of spiritual develop-
ment. Dipa-Ma was a little bundle of a woman wrapped in
a white sari, but her psychic space was huge, radiating light
and peace, filling whatever room she was in. To visit her, I
had to make my way past piles of garbage in the alley en
route to the dim, narrow staircase that climbed to her tiny
Calcutta apartment. There I often found her sitting cross-
legged on the wooden bed in the corner of her room. Invariably, she smiled, radiating a calm in total contrast to the
shrieks of neighboring metal-grinding shops and the frantic
streets below.

Greeting me, Dipa-Ma would take my head in her hands,
stroke my hair, and whisper, "May you be happy, may you be
peaceful." Then over tea, as we discussed my meditation
practice, she would gently push me beyond my self-imposed
limits. "You can do it." "Sit longer." "Be more diligent." As I
sat at her feet, basking in her loving presence, I longed to be
like her. If only I could be so strong yet loving, so able to
rise above my circumstances.

No matter which teacher I was near in those days, I lost
myself in admiration. In the glow of bright faith, I believed
whatever they said without question. But bright faith doesn't
last. Like a crush on our fourth-grade teacher, bright faith

is meant to be a prelude to a more mature regard, in which love for the other is investigated and balanced by our own self-respect. For our faith to mature, we need to weigh what others tell us against our own experience of the truth. We need to honor ourselves enough to rely on our own experiences more than on the experiences of others.

When we place our faith entirely in others, rather than remembering the need for faith in our own understanding, we end up caught in the shadow side of surrender and devotion. Whatever relationships we form, whether with a friend or lover or coworker or teacher or doctrine, will be passive and dependent, leaving us afraid to question, afraid of being unable to see clearly for ourselves, afraid of being left out, of being challenging. We may subvert reason, intelligence, and whatever else we have in order to keep someone as the repository of our trust.

For faith to be balanced it is vital that we examine closely the recipient of our heart, because delivered with our heart is our life's energy. To offer the heart is not like offering a fingernail or a lock of hair we were ready to discard anyway; it is to offer the core, most essential part of our being. To offer the heart with full respect for the power of that offering means looking intently and carefully at where it is going.

In Buddhism, the process of examining in a critical and discriminating way the teacher or teaching that awakened bright faith is called "verifying faith." This is a crucial step of verifying or validating through our own experience what we previously have only heard of or seen outside ourselves. The Buddha likened this process of investigation to the method for analyzing gold. The gold is scorched with fire, then cut and rubbed to test its purity. Likewise, we test the attractive, shiny allure of bright faith by examination, to see if the teachings hold up in our lives. In this way we learn to trust our own experience of the truth rather than an abstract tradition or authority.

It is a common assumption that faith deepens as we are taught more about what to believe; in Buddhism, on the contrary, faith grows only as we question what we are told, as we try teachings out by putting them into practice to see if they really make a difference in our own lives. The Buddha himself insisted, "Don't believe anything just because I have said it. Don't believe anything just because an elder or someone you respect has said it. Put it into practice. See for yourself if it is true." I felt a growing excitement at what I was learning about the relationship of the body and mind, about the power of concentration, about the laws of nature and change. But many of those new ideas, though they struck me as true, were not yet my own experience. I *believed* what I was hearing but hadn't proven the truth of it to myself. To move from the floating world of bright faith to the more solid ground of verified faith I would have to ask questions, find a voice, explore the teachings for myself. Rather than asking me to adopt a set of customs and beliefs, Buddhism has led me over and over again back to the even more decided challenge of finding out what is true for myself. The path of faith being held out to me in those early days in India was more alive, riskier, and certainly more liberating than I had ever imagined.

However, the injunction to "find out for yourself" ran headlong into the adaptive stance of my childhood, which was to avoid direct involvement and keep my distance. My paternal grandparents, with whom I lived after my mother's death, were Eastern European immigrants, uneasy with speaking of upsetting topics. The dominant mode of communication was to shun unpleasantness or to repackage it in a more acceptable format. No one at home seemed capable of saying the words "dying" or even "sick" in a normal tone of voice. If voices dropped to a whisper as I walked into a room, I pretty much knew my deceased mother or my still-absent father was being discussed. I held tightly to myself the questions that filled my mind. "Where is my father?" "Why isn't he here?" "What do I say to people at school who ask?"

By the time my father reappeared, he had been out of my life for seven years. When he took an overdose of sleeping pills six weeks later and was put into an institution, I was told it was simply an accident. In my isolation I had no way of coming to terms with his depression, or his desire to die, or the terrible secret fear within me that it was somehow really my fault. Not until I was in college—five years later—did it strike me how unusual it was that an "accident" with pills could land someone in a mental hospital indefinitely.

Any of us brought up with or subject to such instability learn how to avoid rocking the boat and trying to ferret out the deeper truth of any situation. Better just to be quiet and at least preserve an illusion of stability and belonging. Anything threatening fills us with anxiety, so that our facility to ask questions, to seek answers, along with having confidence in our right to know, ends up frozen.

At those early retreats led by Goenka, I sat quietly in the back of the meditation hall, watching and listening as other students eagerly questioned him. Every evening after his lecture we gathered for informal discussion that went on until he finally sent us to get some sleep. Ignited by the excitement of discovery, people fired off question after question. "Do I have to believe in rebirth in order to do this practice?" "What did the Buddha mean that attachment causes suffering? Attachment seems to make me happy." "Why all this emphasis on suffering? It's too depressing." "If I think negative thoughts about other people, will I hurt them?" "Will I get permanent bliss if I meditate every day?"

Even thinking about speaking up, as I saw so many others doing, had me wanting to curl up inside myself. I would start to raise my hand, and then freeze. A feeling of shame would arise, as though I had neither the ability nor the right to seek answers. In my mind, I didn't have a right to question any more than I had a right to be alive.

There was something else going on as well. Although Goenka was encouraging me to explore and examine the teachings, I see now that what I really wanted was for him to give me the definitive word on what was good and what wasn't, what I could trust and what I couldn't. I wanted to find in Buddhism a system I could belong to. I wanted to be able to say, "I am a Buddhist, and therefore I am compelled to believe the following fifteen things. That's who I am." I was trying desperately to reduce the range of choices life was presenting every single day by making one controlling choice. A belief system might keep all uncertainty and fear away, keep the complexities and ambiguities of the world away.

I had been raised for a time in the orthodox Jewish tradition, where we followed such customs as not turning on lights during the Sabbath and going to temple each week. But I never saw those practices as part of a spiritual path. In my mind they were just family convention and didn't seem to have anything to do with my inner life, which remained a whirlwind of chaos.

Buddhism seemed to promise a way to calm the chaos,

not only through its practices but also, I imagined, by the wholesale adoption of its doctrines. Maybe those beliefs could weave together my shattered sense of self. Maybe if all the answers were given to me, I could find coherence and security in my life. Freud described religious belief systems as forging "a protection against suffering through a delusional remolding of reality." I wanted the protection against suffering so badly that at times I would have happily taken whatever delusional part came with it. When it came down to it, maybe I would rather have followed unthinkingly than have investigated and questioned. It certainly would have been easier.

It's the same longing that seduces people into following ego-centered cult leaders without discrimination. History is rife with the horrors that come with this kind of blind faith. Those on a spiritual path undoubtedly know many stories in which bright faith and blind faith got confused. Dazzled by a teacher or doctrine, we might find ourselves misled, abused, betrayed.

When we fail to question what we are placing our faith in during that first firing of attraction, bright faith becomes blind faith. We stop thinking, we surrender without discernment, we are willing to be deluded as long as we can stay connected to the person or group that stirs our hearts and validates our lives.

One friend of mine got involved with a very charismatic teacher who demanded unquestioning loyalty. My friend soon found that the price of getting close to the teacher's radiant presence was blind surrender. The teacher drew an absolute line between those inside and those outside the group. Outsiders were seen as dangerous. So when an incident happened that would have required discrimination, perhaps dissension, no one was willing to risk exile. Weapons were introduced into the community as a means of protection, but no one, addicted as they were to the teacher's powerful energy, dared question his decision. People were willing to give up their own sense of integrity to enjoy an intoxicating experience.

When faith means complying with someone else's dictates, one either has blind faith or is considered by the authorities to have no faith at all. This was reinforced for me many years after my initial sojourn in India, when I was leading a weekend workshop on the topic of faith and Buddhism. In a beautiful canyon outside of Los Angeles, about fifty people were gathered, sitting on a platform under the shade of an old banyan tree. With clear, open vistas stretching for miles, the location was quite apt for discussing the quality of faith.

After opening with some of the classical definitions of faith in Buddhism—to draw near, to place the heart upon, to set forth—I asked if anyone had any questions. Everyone just sat there with no response. As the morning went on, I detected a growing unease as the group continued to meet my comments and invitations to speak with an almost stony silence.

When we reconvened after lunch, a man sitting in the front row of the platform suddenly burst out with, "I came to Buddhism to get away from all this shit!" Then, more calmly, he went on, "For some of us who got faith pounded into our heads when we were young, it brings up a lot of misgivings." With that the group came alive, and person after person expressed their painful associations with "faith."

Many felt they had been forced to believe something that couldn't be proven, and they had been discouraged from asking questions. "The authorities within my religion were very annoyed when I asked, 'How do you know?'" one woman told the group. "They would just say, 'Have faith,' and I never could. Pretty soon I didn't have any faith at all."

Many had been hurt by the religious teachings of their childhood, in which their degree of faith was the measure of their belonging; if they did not have enough there was something wrong with them or they would be condemned, maybe forevermore. Separating faith from intelligent inquiry casts it as a practice of the gullible.

For a number of people in that workshop, "lack of faith" in their childhood had meant having questions, being uncertain, or maybe even delighting in some aspects of their religious doctrine but not others. Essentially, what they had been denied in their experience with religious beliefs was the sense that they had the right to discover the truth for themselves. They didn't lack faith; they lacked the opportunity to *verify* their faith by examining their beliefs.

If faith depends on believing what we are told, when those beliefs fall apart, we are left with nowhere to stand. A friend of mine began to feel uncomfortable maintaining the Santa Claus myth with her growing daughter, and decided to tell her the truth. She explained that the presents under the tree on Christmas morning were put there by her parents. The child listened to this information, then sadly left the room. A few minutes later she returned to inquire, "Are you the tooth fairy, too?" Her mother said yes, and again the child left, looking sad. Soon she returned with the question, "Are you the Easter bunny as well?" When her mother said yes, the child looked at her fiercely and demanded, "Is there a God?"

For many of us, our inquiry into the nature of life has led to that same predicament: How and when do we trust something as true? What beliefs about life and death are woven into our view of the world? Do these beliefs reflect truth, and can we count on them? If the beliefs crumble, are we bereft of all refuge? Does critical exploration of our beliefs leave us vulnerable and unsure? How can we wholeheartedly have faith rather than a handful of beliefs?

In Buddhism, the distinction between faith and beliefs

lies in testing what we are told. "Put it into practice," the Buddha said, "and if you find that it leads to a kind of wisdom that is like looking at a wall, and then the wall breaks open and you see in a much more unbounded way, then you can trust it." No matter what my teachers told me, it was still a belief until I tried it.

One of the basic teachings in the meditation practice is that focusing on the breath calms the mind. For most of my first retreat I doubted this was true, primarily because I found it so hard to focus on the breath. When I sat I could hear Goenka's voice in my head saying, "When your attention wanders, gently bring it back to the breath. Start again." Even though my thoughts continued to be turbulent, I kept on trying, again and again. Then one day my attention stabilized, and my mind settled into an extraordinary peace. Though that faded away in the natural course of events, because everything does change, I felt I could have faith in this aspect of the practice because I had begun to verify it myself. If this step worked, I reasoned, then maybe I could verify my faith that meditation would indeed lead to wisdom, freedom from suffering, and greater love.

In order to deepen our faith, we have to be able to try things out, to wonder, to doubt. In fact, faith is strengthened by doubt when doubt is a sincere, critical questioning combined with deep trust in our own right and ability to discern the truth. In Buddhism this kind of questioning is known as skillful doubt. For doubt to be skillful we have to be close enough to an issue to care about it, yet open enough to let questioning come alive.

Unlike skillful doubt, which brings us closer to exploring the truth, unskillful doubt pulls us farther away. A story from the Buddha's life illustrates the consequences of unskillful doubt. After his enlightenment, the Buddha arose from his place under the bodhi tree and set out walking along the road. The first person he encountered was struck by the radiance of his face and the power of his presence. Dazzled, the man asked, "Who are you?" The Buddha replied, "I am an awakened one." The man just said, "Well, maybe," and walked away. Had he shown curiosity, then taken the time to follow up on his doubt by asking questions, he might have discovered something profoundly transforming.

This kind of "walk away" doubt manifests as cynicism. Cynicism is actually a self-protective mechanism. A cynical stance allows us to feel smart and unthreatened without really being involved. We can look sophisticated, and we can remain safe, aloof, and at a distance. Maybe we are frightened and hold ourselves apart from life in order to comment on it, rather than grapple with difficult questions. Perhaps habitual suspicion belittles all dreams of change until they simply fade and we no longer believe any change to be possible. We feel impervious and confident, knowing that we're not gullible, we're not going to be swayed.

The cynic not only doubts, however, but also refuses to investigate the object of that doubt. Rather than engaging a person or a problem, the cynic says, "What does that have to do with me?" Like the man who met the Buddha and walked away, the cynic says, "Prove it," without bothering to stick around to question, to see just what proof might be forthcoming.

Sometimes unskillful doubt manifests in what seems on the surface to be sincere questioning, but underneath, the play of endless abstraction is still leaving the questioner uninvolved. That day I was teaching in Los Angeles, the students went on to argue vigorously the existence of a personal, theistic God—a theological discussion that led nowhere because there was no final way to answer it. I wondered, during the whole long, dry duration of the argument, how much the personal pain of any of their lives was being held at bay. Perhaps the unhappiness of a fractured family was staying unaddressed, or maybe an intense need to find forgiveness was being sidelined.

The tendency to fixate on big, unanswerable questions—"Is there a God?" "How does karma work?" "Was there a beginning to the universe?" was characterized as "a desert, a jungle, a puppet show, the writhing entanglement of speculation" by the Buddha. Our obsessions with such questions would lead only to personal resentments and sorrow, not to wisdom or peace, he said. Whenever feverish disputes on such issues rose up around him, instead of joining in and offering a theoretical answer, he urged everyone to find answers for themselves, in a way that would help them resolve the suffering in their lives. To arrive at that resolution of suffering is the point of skillful doubt.

A woman once went to my friend and colleague Sylvia Boorstein in profound dismay over what seemed to be the Buddha's comments on women. Although the woman had great faith in the teachings about life she had heard in Buddhism, she now had great doubts about the Buddha himself. She had heard that when a group of women first asked to become nuns, the Buddha refused them. According to the texts, he replied that if he were to create an order of nuns, the teachings of Buddhism would not last as long in the course of history.

Sylvia began by suggesting that the Buddha's initial refusal might have been a comment on the society of the time and how people would react to women being ordained rather than evidence of bias against women per se. The woman was still very upset. Sylvia then noted that the texts attributed to the Buddha were not even written down until three hundred years after the time of his death, so that this passage may not have reflected him as much as commentaries by monks centuries later who had an ax to grind on the subject. The student was still upset. Finally Sylvia said to her, "So maybe the Buddha was wrong about women and right about suffering."

Both aspects of Sylvia's response reflect the heart of Buddhism: One aspect points us back to the essence of spiritual life being our own exploration of teachings that might help resolve suffering, and the other, in the spirit of "Don't believe anything just because I say it," admits, "Maybe he was wrong about something."

In fact, even the Buddha's attendant Ananda felt free to suggest this. Uncomfortable about the Buddha's reluctance to admit women to the monastic order, Ananda asked if there were any reason women couldn't become enlightened as quickly and easily as men. When the Buddha said "no," Ananda responded, "Well then, why can't they join the order?" At that point, the Buddha agreed to admit them.

The Buddha encouraged people not to simply defer to his authority. Sariputra, one of the chief disciples of the Buddha, was questioned about a doctrine in the Buddha's teaching. In reply Sariputra said, "In this matter, I don't rely on faith in the Buddha." People overhearing his response considered it disrespectful and were very upset—except for the Buddha himself, who told them, "It's good that he relies on his own understanding."

If we feel the Buddha, or any other spiritual leader, is

wrong about something, the most skillful response is to ask ourselves, "How wrong?" Is the teacher condoning violence against women or exploitation of anyone? Are his or her students being wrapped in a cloth of insularity so that the teacher's bias is never challenged? Is there anything in the teacher's system worth learning, even if we discard the rest? What if we were to strip away the social tenets of the Buddha's day, the accretions of 2,500 years of interpretation, and the accumulated belief systems, often trapped in history and culture? Does anything of value remain for us?

Actually we can't know what the Buddha really said about admitting women to monastic life. From other comments attributed to him and from his willingness to openly share the teachings without regard to gender or caste, for the India of his time he seemed revolutionary in his respect for women and others who were powerless in society. If in fact he did make this comment about the order of nuns, we can't know why. What we can know is whether the path of practice he offers leads to the end of suffering or whether it is valuable for us.

My teacher Dipa-Ma is an example of someone who freed her mind from suffering through Buddhist meditation, yet at the same time felt free to challenge elements of Buddhist tradition with which she didn't agree. Dr. Jack Engler, a psychologist and Buddhist teacher, tells the story of a time when he was in India doing research and went to visit Dipa-Ma. He was in her room one day along with Munindra. Dipa-Ma hadn't been feeling well and was sitting on her wooden bed leaning against the wall, her eyes half closed. Munindra was recounting a point from the Buddhist commentaries (that is, something attributed not to the Buddha himself but to later adherents) saying that only men could become buddhas—to become a buddha you had to have taken rebirth as a man. In response Dipa-Ma bolted upright, opened her eyes, and declared without hesitation, "I can do anything a man can do."

I know for a fact that Dipa-Ma thanked the Buddha every day of her life for the techniques he offered that had so helped her. She took the practices to heart yet was willing to question elements of the historical beliefs. She saw that the beliefs were extraneous to what she could have faith in—her ability to reach the liberation the Buddha was talking about. Her experience of transformation was the still center of her faith.

This is the essential questioning we must bring to any belief system: Can it transform our minds? Can it help reshape our pain into wisdom and love? When we grapple with the truth of our experience in relationship to our beliefs, we have the chance to deepen our faith. Does our experience match the belief system or not? If not, we can let the belief go. If it does, we can trust it as our own.

. . .

NOT THAT BELIEFS are necessarily wrong or irrelevant. Every religion, including Buddhism, has a set of beliefs. If they are skillful, beliefs can serve as a reminder of what we value. If we believe in future lives, for example, we may use that as an inspiration not to make a mess out of this life, since habits of discord, strife, and isolation may carry over into the next one. Beliefs can provide a thread of continuity and perspective as we undergo the tumultuous changes and storms of everyday life.

It's not the existence of beliefs that is the problem, but what happens to us when we hold them rigidly, without examining them, when we presume the absolute centrality of our views and become disdainful of others. Placing ourselves in a position of privilege—beliefs are treasured commodities and we are the proud owners—implies that we alone possess the earth, we possess the Truth. In a spirit of magnanimity we might look kindly at those who don't share our views, but they remain the "other," and we don't really need to listen to them. *Our* story becomes *the* story. The smugness that ensues is so quietly assumed, it is no longer like an article of clothing we put on: It is skeletal. This kind of certainty can't tolerate being questioned and must dismiss any kind of confrontation. Meaningful and honest discussion of an issue might be overridden: "We don't need to talk about that. Don't you trust me? Don't you trust us?"

Taken to an extreme, this self-referential tendency becomes fanaticism. I once went to hear the Dalai Lama give a lecture where there were people outside carrying placards that proclaimed, "Accept Jesus or you'll go to hell!" They patrolled the entryway, as if patrolling the boundaries of reality, screaming their message at each of us who walked past them. Buddhists are not immune to rigidly holding on to beliefs and using them as means to display superiority. This kind of attachment and derision, ironically, contradicts the basic tenets of Buddhism.

Buddhism uses an analogy to describe what happens when we allow fixed beliefs to contour reality for us. Buddhists say that holding such views is like gazing at the sky through a straw. The sky is the unobstructed truth of who we are and what our lives are about. When a received belief system circumscribes that for us, it is as if we are looking at the truth through a narrow tube, seeing only a very small part of it while convinced we are seeing the whole. When we're attached to our beliefs, we can spend a lot of time comparing straws: "I've got a better straw than you. It's a little wider and it's got a design on it." Especially in the face of fear, we tend to hold on to our straws with a death grip.

When I first began teaching meditation with Joseph Goldstein at Naropa University in Boulder, Colorado, I had very little self-confidence. I was twenty-one years old and much younger than most of the people I was teaching. To hide my fear I answered questions with great conviction, quoting from text and tradition but not really knowing the answers from my own experience. When traditions clashed, I was in trouble.

I had practiced largely in the context of Theravada Buddhism, which is preserved in Burma, Thailand, and other countries of Southeast Asia. Naropa University was founded by Trungpa Rinpoche, who was Tibetan, and the teaching in most classes was within the Tibetan tradition, which is aligned with Mahayana Buddhism. The Theravadan view of what happens after death is quite different from the Tibetan view. While the Theravadans say that one dies and is reborn in the very next moment, the Tibetans say that one goes through the phases of a *bardo,* an intermediate stage, before rebirth.

For four years I had been steeped in the Theravadan tradition, used its language and idioms, and heard its stories and myths again and again. I had been acculturated to that point of view. So one day when someone from the Tibetan tradition challenged me about what really happens after death, I responded stridently, clinging to my Theravadan straw. He and I were all alone in a sparsely furnished room. As we argued vociferously, each insisting on the rightness of our different views of the after-death state, the room grew full with our opinions and increasing dislike of each other. The man got angrier and angrier as I persisted in casting a picture quite different from his. Finally, he lost his temper and, yelling, accused me of being a liar. In a way he was right. I had no real knowledge of what happens after death, no matter what any tradition says, and I was too afraid to simply say, "I don't know."

When we hold a belief too tightly, it is often because we are afraid. We become rigid, and chastise others for believing the wrong things without really listening to what they are saying. We become defensive and resist opening our minds to new ideas or perspectives. This doesn't mean that all beliefs are accurate reflections of the truth, but it does mean that we have to look at what's motivating our defensiveness. Confronted with the vastness of the sky, and unsure where safety lies, we often seek refuge in our own very special straw. The mind's determination to see things a certain way transforms fear into hostility. It is likely that the man at Naropa University and I were fundamentally just two people afraid to die.

Whether there is a bardo or instant rebirth was not as central to our lives as the fact that for both of us there would come a moment when we would have to let go of absolutely everything—body, mind, friends, enemies, all that we cherish, all that we know. It's a lot easier to argue about particular beliefs from a sectarian point of view than it is to look at our primal level of fear. That man and I were caught in what we thought we knew, and were unable to open in faith to what was beyond our insistence. If both of us could have gotten into questioning, wondering, we might have arrived at what we had faith in as essential to face the catastrophic letting go of death. If we had been able to hold our beliefs more skillfully, we might have seen that we can question our beliefs freely without fear of losing our faith.

With their assumptions of correctness, beliefs try to make a known out of the unknown. They make presumptions about what is yet to come, how it will be, what it will mean, and how it will affect us. Faith, on the other hand, doesn't carve out reality according to our preconceptions and desires. It doesn't decide how we are going to perceive something but rather is the ability to move forward even without knowing. Faith, in contrast to belief, is not a definition of reality, not a received answer, but an active, open state that makes us willing to explore. While beliefs come to us from outside—from another person or a tradition or heritage—faith comes from within, from our alive participation in the process of discovery.

Writer Alan Watts summed up the difference simply and pointedly as, "Belief clings, faith lets go." As I matured in practice and teaching, I found the confidence to say more often, with greater ease, "The tradition says such and such,

but I myself don't know." Rather than hiding behind a belief
system, I was revealing a growing acceptance of entering
the unknown, dwelling in the unknown, bearing the unknown. I was depending on my faith rather than beliefs. I
was learning how to let go of my rigid grip on the straw.

Once, I went to an interfaith conference at which eminent representatives of different traditions were presenting
their views on topics such as suffering, effort, and faith.
One of the most striking moments of the event came at the
end, when one of the speakers pointed out that whenever
the Dalai Lama spoke, he qualified his remarks by saying,
"From the Buddhist point of view, it is . . ." or at times by
referring to a particular Buddhist philosophical stance,
"From the Madhyamika point of view, it is . . ." In contrast,
she noted, many speakers had simply declared with some
fervor, "It is . . ." There were varied straws being presented
at the conference, but the Dalai Lama was keeping in mind
the centrality of the sky.

When we have the courage to put down the straw and
view the sky as it is, vast and unimpeded, then we can recognize the varied perspectives each straw gives us. We can
recognize the difference between our very favorite straw,
our most accustomed straw, our exquisitely preserved straw,
and the sky itself. If we hold the straw skillfully, we will be
able to put it down sometimes and look nakedly at the sky.
If we hold beliefs skillfully, we will not get entangled in

them, but will see them as the mental constructs they are. When we claim our right to question everything, including our beliefs, we can unhook from our dependence on what is familiar and let in the heartfelt, open, fresh quality of faith.

As I continued to meditate, I began to recognize that my desire to accept whatever doctrine was given arose out of doubts about myself and my abilities. Regardless of the beliefs to which I subscribed, that was the area I would have to heal. I would have to think enough of myself to claim the right to question what was offered, to investigate what I was being told, to trust my own experience. To do that would mean confronting years of habit, of closing down when I felt insecure. The first crack in my shell was awkward and unsure, but it was a significant step in deepening my understanding, so that what I had faith in could be more than just something I blindly accepted or went along with.

After I had been meditating in India for months, one evening at another ten-day course with Goenka, I reached the end of my rope. I felt exhilarated at each nightly lecture, and happy to be in Goenka's presence, but the inner potential that the Buddha claimed was universal seemed very far away. My back was aching, again. Instead of experiencing peace of mind, I was beset by repetitive and trivial thoughts. Instead of doing the practice—which depended upon being in the moment in order to liberate myself from the unconscious patterns of the past—I was lost in the future most of the day. I planned umpteen years ahead. I wrote and rewrote letters home in my mind, carefully fitting my words about meditation practice into the limited space of an imaginary aerogram. Restless and agitated, I considered in great detail the pros and cons of a trip to Thailand, or maybe Burma, their hot seasons, rainy seasons, and the difficulties of getting the required inoculations. Every once in a while I would wake up, realize I'd been lost, and despair of finding any inner peace. As I noticed myself planning for the hundredth time a trip to town to buy some cloth, I felt hammered by the banality of my own mind.

The honeymoon was over. I couldn't see an end to the difficulty and, in fact, I'd lost sight of the point of practicing at all. That night, beleaguered, I got up from my place at the back of the hall and moved to the front. I sat down facing Goenka, in the first row of students. To cut off his most persistent student, who had dominated the scene each night, I squeezed in even closer to Goenka. Ignoring the student's upstretched arm as he vied to get in another question, I took a deep breath, looked Goenka in the eye, and in the presence of all those dozens of people, blurted out, "Isn't there an easier way?" It was as if I suspected that if I could only catch him off guard, he would be forced to admit that he knew a far easier way to freedom, but preferred to torment his students by withholding it.

On one level I knew it was an absurd question: Goenka was far too kind to toy with us. But it was very important for me to ask it anyway. My fledgling ability to question had finally allowed me to express doubt—about him, about the practice, about the path. I had begun to deepen my faith by risking the coming close that is at the heart of skillful questioning. Goenka, looking delighted, simply laughed and said, "If I knew it, I'd tell you." He didn't try to justify his teaching style, but then, he didn't need to. He knew that for me to see the pain and agitation within was a big step toward becoming free of it. I'm sure he knew, too, how important it was that I was determined to experience the truth directly, rather than have it be an intellectual exercise or an abstract delight.

It was the beginning of a state of mind in which I felt more empowered to discover for myself what was true. Questioning what was being told to me, both doctrinally and in terms of meditation instruction, translated into the right attitude for meditation practice—looking at all experience without prior assumptions, with enough courage to examine everything, for a personal, direct knowledge of the truth. If we just accept concepts mindlessly, our relationship to them loses vigor; if we question them, they become vibrant and alive. I would go on inquiring, internally and externally, until many concepts were filled with the life-force of my participation, my engagement, my faith.

Asking questions to find truth goes far beyond learning to more freely question others. It means adopting an attitude of wonder, delving into whatever is in front of us, in order to taste and touch and feel it acutely for ourselves and learn from it. It means investigating and exploring, knowing we have the ability to find out for ourselves what can free our minds and make us happy. With the power that comes uniquely from our own experience, we discover what we can wholeheartedly put our faith in rather than hold tenuously as belief.

Questioning means longing to know the truth deeply, and insisting that we can. It means leaving whatever distant slant we may occupy to come close and see more directly what is true. And it means being willing to be honest about how we ourselves are seeing things, even if that vision differs from the norm. Learning to question means feeling we have the innate right to all of this.

For faith to be alive and to deepen we need to use our power to inquire, to wonder, to explore our experience to see what is true for ourselves. This requires us to approach life with an inquisitive, eager, self-confident capacity to probe and question. It requires us to examine where we place our faith, and why, to see if it makes us more aware and loving people. To develop a verified faith we need to open to the messiness, the discordance, the ambivalence, and, above all, the vital life-force of questioning. If we don't, our faith can wither. If we don't, our faith will always remain in the hands of someone else, as something we borrow or abjure, but not as something we can claim fully as our own.

CHAPTER 4

faith and fear

A FEW WINTERS AGO there was a major exhibit
of Vincent van Gogh's artwork at the Los Angeles County
Museum of Art. The paintings included both exuberant out-
pourings and canvases tinged with foreboding. As I walked
through the museum, my feelings kept shifting. What I found
most heartrending in van Gogh's work were the contrasts,
the intensity of the swings from one mood to another. The
paintings of "light"—sun-drenched landscapes, still lifes of
flowering branches, the bedroom at Arles—were tender,
renewing, beckoning. Other, darker canvases—of twilight,
ominous skies—drew me into his vortex of sorrow.

I imagined how van Gogh must have so poignantly
grieved a mood's passing, as the light went and the darkness
descended once more. I envisioned him engulfed by his
changing states, with no refuge, no place to go to get per-

74

spective or feel safe. A close friend of mine was in the midst of a major bout of depression. Another had been hospitalized for the past several months with recurrent pneumonia, as well as a puzzling disease physician after physician was unable to diagnose. I stood in front of van Gogh's painting *Wheatfield with Crows,* thinking of the artist, of my friends, of myself—how all of us face the ungovernable nature of life and the suffering that comes from our powerlessness, our inability to stop the changes. Every day we might think that we have it all under control, only to once again suffer defeat.

I turned from the painting and set off for the museum gift shop to meet a friend. The shop was packed with people and souvenirs of the exhibit. At one point I found myself wedged between a pile of Vincent van Gogh pool towels and a display of Vincent van Gogh mouse pads. The contrast between my experience in the exhibit and what surrounded me in the gift shop was bizarre. As if the vast, untamable flow of life I'd seen evidenced in van Gogh's paintings could be captured and neatly packaged into manageable and marketable items—pool towels and mouse pads and umbrellas—to be bought, wrapped up, and tucked away. Nevertheless, for a moment I, too, was tempted to buy a souvenir that might serve as a totem against an out-of-control world.

The fact is that nothing we acquire—not even a Vincent van Gogh mouse pad today and a pool towel tomorrow—will put conditions under our command. Life is like an ever-shifting kaleidoscope—a slight change, and all patterns and configurations alter. A fight with a friend causes fifteen other relationships to stir and turn, our lives interconnected like a game of dominoes. One moment everything feels full and perfect—the next an accident happens or we fall sick. Settled comfortably into being single, we meet someone and fall deeply in love. We are going along in one direction when an unforeseen obstacle appears, and we have to swerve out of the way. Suddenly, stunningly, we are in a different life.

NO MATTER how much we want it to be otherwise, the truth is that we are not in control of the unfolding of our experiences. Despite our search for stability and prediction, for the center of our lives to hold firm, it never does. Life is wilder than that—a flow we can't command or stave off. We can affect and influence and impact what happens, but we can't wake up in the morning and decide what we will encounter and feel and be confronted by during the day.

Invariably, when I think I have finally gotten some aspect of myself under control, life intrudes forcefully to show me otherwise. During the winter of the Vincent van

Gogh mouse pads, I came down with a bad case of flu. Nevertheless I continued to travel and teach until the flu turned to bronchitis so severe that I broke a rib coughing. One evening, when I was on the verge of another relapse, some friends took me to an outdoor mineral bath—supposedly healing waters.

We sat together in the warm water for some time, looking at the stars, enjoying easy, rambling talk. After a while the topic turned to fear, and how often it arises when we realize we aren't in control of events. We each told stories of when we had faced fear and how we had handled it, gracefully or poorly. Almost nonchalantly I commented, "It feels like it has been a long time since I had an experience of acute, intense fear—fear right down to my bones." Because of the greater serenity I had developed through meditation, I actually thought I had fear under control, that it was something I used to deal with, long ago, in my distant past. In terms of debilitating, crushing fear, I believed, "Never again."

Just two hours later my bronchitis turned to asthma—the first asthma attack of my life. Lying down, trembling, unable to breathe, I wondered if I was in fact dying. The air around me seemed to have changed to a viscous substance too thick to inhale. An astounding primal, physical anxiety coursed through me. As I gasped for air, an image of my friend in the hospital with pneumonia came to mind, and I had a sudden, terrible conviction that he would die. Overwhelmed by the vision of someone struggling futilely to breathe, struggling until death, I realized that could also be me. Sure enough, the fear went right down to my bones.

Psychiatrist P. W. Winnicott once alluded to those moments in which we are utterly helpless as the feeling of falling endlessly. Winnicott used this image to describe the experience of growing up under the care of a depressed mother, but it is also one that describes what any of us might feel when no one seems to be in charge, when a situation we've relied on is coming apart, when everything around us is spinning out of control.

Like most people, I'd been trained to fear anything I couldn't control: the unruly emotions of my mind, the unreliable character of my body, uncultivated nature, and certainly physical death, as well as all the little echoes of death that appear in everyday change. It might have felt safer avoiding or denying the fierce uncertainty, the volcanic underpinnings of life. But as I learned to see with less illusion, I began to accept that, no matter how I felt about it, life would never become predictable and orderly and fixed. I had to find something other than fear to guide me.

For most of us, when life feels out of control our most ready response is fear. When fear dominates, our sense of possibility collapses. Many years ago I attended a stress-reduction program led by Jon Kabat-Zinn. In one exercise, he stepped up to the blackboard and in the center drew a square made up of nine dots, arranged in three parallel lines with three dots in each line. Then he challenged everyone in the class to take the piece of chalk and see if we could connect all the dots using only four straight lines, without removing the chalk from the blackboard, and without re-tracing a line. One by one, all thirty of us went up to the blackboard. We tried beginning from the left, from the right, from the top, from the bottom, and returned to our seats frustrated, unable to do what he'd asked. The room was vibrating with stress.

Then Jon picked up the chalk and with great sweeping strokes that extended well beyond the perimeter of the small square, did exactly what he had challenged us to do. Every one of us had presumed that to succeed we had to stay within the circumscribed area formed by the nine dots. Jon had never said that we were limited to that little space, but all of us had concluded that was the only area in which we had to move, in which to find options. Not one of us could see beyond our assumptions.

Fear makes that same kind of assumption. It limits our options, strangles creativity, restricts our vision of what is possible. When the danger is physical, fear leads us in one of two directions: fight or flight. The body mobilizes to help us battle the menace or flee to safety. But even when we aren't in mortal danger, if we're lost in fear we respond the same way. We either resist what is happening by angrily insisting that it be different, or we tighten up and pull away, denying our experience. When we are deeply afraid, we view any change as a threat and the unfamiliar as a mortal enemy.

Being alive necessarily means uncertainty and risk, times of going into the unknown. If we withdraw from the flow of life, our hearts contract. We hold back so much that we feel separate from our own bodies and minds, separate from other people, even people we really care about. In the grip of other intense emotions, like grief and jealousy, we might feel anguish, but fear shuts us down, arrests the life-force. To be driven by fear is like dying inside.

When the suffering is overwhelming, we may try to recoil from how bad it feels by numbing our reactions. Many of us survived childhood in just this way. But, ultimately, cutting ourselves off from what is happening locks us into fear and makes us unable to see that we might find another way to respond outside the small section delineated by the dots, defined by our assumptions.

Faith, in contrast, reminds us of the ever-changing flow of life, with all its movement and possibility. Faith is the capacity of the heart that allows us to draw close to the present and find there the underlying thread connecting the moment's experience to the fabric of all of life. It opens us to a bigger sense of who we are and what we are capable of doing.

To act with faith, however, means not getting seduced by any of its ready replacements. One of the most subtle ways fear can bind us, so quietly that we hardly know to call it fear, is what is known in Buddhist teachings as "fixated hope." Fixated hope, like hope itself, resembles faith in that both sparkle with a sense of possibility. But fixated hope is conditional, circumscribing happiness to getting what we want. We may, for example, have faith in our children's ability to have a meaningful life, but if to us that means they will grow up to be doctors or lawyers rather than custodians or waiters, what we are really doing is trying to manage life. Any insistence that people or circumstances meet our exact expectations is not faith but another effort at control, bound to end in disappointment.

I am not at all suggesting hopelessness. It's natural to want things to work out in ways that we believe will be for the good. When we are in pain, hoping for things to be another way can be essential to our health and even our survival. When we're unhappy, it is natural to picture how things might be better. True hope can open our hearts and remind us of light when we are in darkness. But when our hope for relief from suffering is based only on getting what we want, in the precise way we want it, we bind hope to fear rather than to faith.

Buddhism regards fixated hope and fear as two sides of the same coin. When we hope for a particular outcome to arise or a desire to be met, we invariably fear that it won't happen. Thus we move from hope to fear to hope to fear to hope to fear in an endless loop. Fixated hope promises to break us free of the circumscribed area in the middle of the blackboard, only to lead us right back to the narrow confines of that little square.

I saw myself caught in this cycle of hope and fear when Ram Dass, Western spiritual teacher and author, suffered a massive stroke in 1997. He is an old and close friend of mine. Starting with our first Buddhist meditation retreat in Bodhgaya, India, he and I often pursued spiritual practice together in many places around the world. We loved and respected many of the same teachers. A close confidant, Ram Dass once helped me through a long and difficult relationship breakup. We had a rich and ongoing dialogue on issues such as the role of spiritual awareness in social change. We also celebrated many of our significant life passages together, such as his sixtieth birthday. We had been fond of each other for decades.

During the hours immediately following news of his stroke, a few of our mutual friends gathered at my house. Not knowing if Ram Dass would live or die, not knowing to what extent he might ever recover speech and mobility, we were all trying to comfort one another. We meditated, we reminisced, we waited for news, and we speculated. Fear spiked through my body. I was in shock, and was scared of the pictures that kept entering my mind. Obsessing over what might happen, I replayed each scenario a dozen times: "Maybe he'll be able to speak again but not walk. Maybe he will be able to write but not speak. Maybe he will make a complete recovery." Clearly this was all conjecture, a way of trying to gain some control over the situation—as if by repeating something enough times I could make it happen.

I wanted Ram Dass to recover from the stroke looking and acting just the way he had looked and acted before. I wanted him walking, funny, brilliant. I might have called my response true hope, but it was actually fixated hope. Fear kept me from letting in the reality: Ram Dass was immobile, unable to communicate, facing an uncertain outcome.

Frustrated that I couldn't do anything about the situation, I prayed. I called on all the buddhas and bodhisattvas of the universe, those beings who represent freedom to me, who are the embodiment of goodness and wisdom. I was reaching out for refuge, and this time I wasn't looking for support from the buddha-mind within me. I was joining all those who call out to the Buddha in devotion. I was seeking shelter and support, and my request was urgent.

Turning to something bigger and more powerful made me feel less alone, and more aligned with forces of protection and love. But I still felt anxious. Finally I had to admit that I wasn't really placing the situation in the arms of the

Buddha. I was fervently praying that this disaster would all just go away, that Ram Dass would be completely well, as if the stroke had never happened. Or maybe he could be even better. I was praying for things to go exactly the way I wanted them to.

Praying like this isn't a bad practice. When I was in the hospital facing surgery and a potential malignancy, my friend Sylvia Boorstein prayed for me. She later told me, "I didn't do any of that 'Whatever may be in her best interests, may it come to pass' stuff. I just said, 'No cancer! Got that, God?' " I laughed hard at her spiritual "political incorrectness." It felt great to be so powerfully supported by the intensity of her caring. I believe that such prayers generate an energy that can have an effect. I also enjoyed her unabashed willingness to admit that she had strong desires about what should happen for me, and that she wanted the outcome exactly as she was stating it, no deviations allowed. Got that, God?

But Sylvia knew—as I did in praying for Ram Dass— that if we absolutely insist that things work out only as we want them to, our prayers become a version of fixated hope. When hope and prayer become strategies to avoid facing what is, then we have nothing on which to base either effective action or real peace of mind. We're back in the hope/fear dilemma.

When I saw the reason for my anxiety, I began to relax.

Outside the limitations of my fear lay a vast space of possibility. I aimed my mind toward it. Underneath my walking/talking/same-as-before agenda, what I really wanted to pray for was that Ram Dass would not feel all alone; that he would feel sheltered and held, that benevolence would surround him. This had nothing to do with demanding a specific outcome. I saw that Ram Dass was going into the unknown, into a realm none of us could control, and if I couldn't accept that, I couldn't go there with him. The more I resented or denied the reality of what was true, the more limited I would be in my ability to support my friend in a loving way.

Throughout the course of that night, I sat side by side with fear. As I acknowledged it, befriending myself despite the fear, my heart began to open. I met the unknown without a strategic plan for control.

With fear no longer dominating my mind, my love for Ram Dass could arise freely. Loving him didn't depend on a fixated hope for his recovery. The power of love wouldn't shatter in the face of change or disintegrate in the wash of my own terror.

We had all fallen silent, each of us with our own thoughts of Ram Dass, when, late into the night, one of his closest friends, Mirabai Bush, quietly spoke. "Here and now we have entered the mystery," she said. "This is a time for faith." As each of us accepted the fact of Ram Dass's stroke and surrendered to our inability to control the situation, tenderness and a tangible peace filled the room. None of us knew what would happen, but faith allowed us to relax into this vast space of *not knowing*. Even as I felt the ache of sorrow, I remembered that life is bigger than its constantly—sometimes drastically—changing circumstances. Looking around the room at all of us gathered there, I cherished the refuge of sangha, community, which has continually helped me open to a greater truth.

My eyes wandered to the mantelpiece in my living room, where there are two photos of my Tibetan Buddhist teacher, Nyoshul Khen Rinpoche, known as Khenpo. They were taken one afternoon in the Catskills when we visited a veterinarian's home together. As we sat and drank tea, a pet dove flew over and landed on Khenpo's hand. One photograph shows him smiling softly as he cradles the dove. In the other picture, the dove has just taken flight and Khenpo is laughing, as if rejoicing in its release. I had gazed at those pictures every day, and as I thought of Ram Dass they felt especially significant. Ram Dass and I had studied together with Khenpo and delighted in the playful nature of this extraordinary teacher. One of the great lessons I learned from Khenpo was the power of letting go in the face of the unexpected changes of life.

In Tibet, Khenpo was a highly regarded teacher. After

his escape from persecution under the Communist Chinese regime, he lived for a time as a beggar on the streets of Calcutta. Through it all, Khenpo's faith in the dharma, the truth of how things are, was unwavering. "Sometimes I was exalted and quite comfortable," he said. "More often I was bereft and poverty-stricken. Yet the inexhaustible wealth of inner truth and peace that is the dharma always sustained me well."

Looking at the photos, I was again inspired by Khenpo's faith. I could take refuge in the dharma, as if I were the dove cradled in Khenpo's hand, trusting that I was held by the quality of love he exhibited. I could also, like Khenpo, let go—and allow the moment to take flight.

Rather than searching for something that would keep me safe from change, I could reach for a home in the shifting shadows and light surrounding me. I couldn't demand Ram Dass's recovery; I couldn't deny that I was afraid for him. But I had a choice between acting out of fear masquerading as hope, or acting with faith.

Faith enables us, despite our fear, to get as close as possible to the truth of the present moment, so that we can offer our hearts fully to it, with integrity. We might (and often must) hope and plan and arrange and try, but faith enables us to be fully engaged while also realizing that we are not in control, and that no strategy can ever put us in control, of the unfolding of events. Faith gives us a willingness to engage life, which means the unknown, and not to shrink back from it.

The English word "courage" has the same etymological root as the French *coeur,* which means "heart." To have courage, just as to have faith, is to be full of heart. With courage we openly acknowledge what we can't control, make wise choices about what we can affect, and move forward into the uncultivated terrain of the next moment.

So it is with faith. That long night, I realized that for me to meet Ram Dass's stroke with faith instead of fear would mean experiencing him fully as he was and as he continued to change. It would mean that if I realized there was little I could do to help him, I wouldn't abandon my friend so as to avoid getting hurt if things didn't go well. With faith I could stay connected to him and not let dismay at my own powerlessness get in the way of my love for him. To act with faith would mean learning to care about Ram Dass in a way not based on language skills, mobility, or even on his staying alive. The closeness, the understanding, the devotion of love wouldn't diminish in letting go, as when Khenpo had let go of the dove.

Just as faith brings us to a steadfast love, the power of love allows us to "faithe." Kierkegaard wrote: "Hope becomes faith through love." By revealing the grace of connection no matter what is happening, love releases us from our efforts to control life. Love opens our hearts wide enough to admit the unknown, the ungovernable. That openness creates the space we need to step outside our restrictive habits and come forward in faith.

I once went to a lecture by a woman who miraculously had begun walking after being long confined to a wheelchair. Across the circle from me, sitting in a wheelchair, was a handsome young man in his early twenties. Beside him sat his father, wearing a work uniform, as if he had hurried there without time to change. The father's shoulders were slumped; he looked worn out. I found my attention riveted to the two men. I watched the hunger in the young man's eyes and wondered if it reflected the depth of his hope to walk again. I watched the love in the father's eyes as he stole glances at his son. I could see the thin sliver of emotion on which the father was balanced, not wanting his son to get his hopes up too high, yet not wanting him to sink lower into resignation. While the man must have wished fervently that his son would walk again, I felt that his love for his son was completely independent of any particular outcome, so that he could be guided by faith instead of fear.

In a similar way, I saw that to tie my love for Ram Dass to my need for his recovery was to fasten an immensity of possibility and connection to a very precarious vehicle— getting what I wanted. Letting go of that need would allow my love for him to open me to faith.

. . .

ABOUT A YEAR after his stroke, Ram Dass and I were
sitting together on his front porch. He had regained a con-
siderable facility in speaking by then, but it was often difficult for him to freely express himself. This was particularly
poignant because before his stroke Ram Dass's eloquence
was his own special magic. His lectures had often been
spellbinding.

Haltingly now, a few labored words at a time, he asked
me how work on my book on faith was going. "It's really
hard," I told him. "I've never had to go so deep inside myself before." Then I realized that what I'd just said wasn't
exactly true. "Actually," I amended, "I've never had to go
so deep inside myself before and bring out the words."
He looked softly at me and slowly said, "That's how . . . I
am . . . every day . . . now."

Having faith doesn't mean that we don't make an effort. When we are trying to create change, we can pour
ourselves into the endeavor and do our best to accomplish
our goal, doing our absolute best to speak, to heal, to create, to alleviate suffering—our own or others'. The particular gift of faith is that it allows us to make that intensity of
effort guided by a more holistic vision of life, with all its
mutability, evanescence, dislocations, and unruliness.

My porch visit with Ram Dass went on through the afternoon. There were long periods of silently being together, listening to the birds, feeling the breeze, being grateful to be alive. Periodically, one or the other of us tried to pull up some words from a deep place inside. At one point, Ram Dass mentioned someone's name, a person known to me as well, who had also had a stroke. "She has lost her faith," he declared. "For thirty years, she believed only . . . in the . . . beneficence of God, and then she had her stroke . . . and then she saw . . ." He looked right at me, and in his eyes I glimpsed the immensity of what he had seen since the stroke. It was like looking at a whole cosmos—of shock and pain and frustration and shame. But unlike that woman, whose picture of life excluded suffering, Ram Dass had opened his worldview wide enough to include it. And so he knew that in that cosmos, alongside pain was gratitude, love, care, and learning to receive. The look in his eyes was so intense, I almost fell over.

I told Ram Dass about what had happened to me the night of his stroke, how I'd had to open beyond my desires, beyond my fears, beyond my longing for neat and recognizable benevolence that would make him all better. Smiling, he said, "It seems . . . I've taught more about love through this stroke . . . than I have through all my thirty years . . . of lecturing about it." He also has taught us about a power of faith that doesn't depend on clinging to the known, but instead on opening to the vastness and mystery of what life provides in each moment.

WHATEVER TAKES US to our edge, to our outer limits, leads us to the heart of life's mystery, and there we find faith. In the process, however, we may have to confront many old habits. When my asthma attack began, my first impulse was to fight against it, to get through it with steely resolve. Flailing against my inability to breathe, I was swept up in the relentless momentum of panic. I was not only afraid, but worse, I was afraid of being afraid. I fought the fear and tangled with it, hating myself for my powerlessness in the face of it. The whirlwind of terror grew, and I pushed against it and pushed against it. The more I tried to resist the fear the stronger it became until, exhausted, I gave up the struggle.

Without the support of my tension and resistance, the fear immediately lessened, and I began to remember insights I'd gained through years of practice: "I don't really know what's happening here." "Beware of that determined slide to the worst possible, barely imaginable scenario." "You don't have to go there. Let's just see what happens now."

I was still afraid, but I wasn't cascading down the slippery slope of trying to claim control and feeling powerless

when I couldn't. I was afraid but I wasn't cut off from remembering the power of being in the moment, and the
possibilities held latent there.

The panic, the grief, the gasping for breath didn't vanish,
but now they seemed to float like buoys on an underlying
calm. The thick atmosphere that had seemed so oppressive
began to thin out. My mind, which had drawn back into
a tight corner of dread, found there was room to move. I
could feel my heart rise up in my chest. Though I still had
fear, I also had faith.

In my mind I could hear the words a friend of mine had
said when he received a terminal diagnosis: "I'm not going
to make an enemy of my own death." If I was going to die, I
didn't want to end my life scalded by my own acrimony at
having failed to wrest control of the situation. If I was going
to live, then I wanted to step out of the trap of an imagined,
assuredly terrible future and reunite with my actual experience in the present. Whatever was happening to me, I
wanted to be fully there for it. In faith, I surrendered to the
moment.

Almost the next instant, it seemed I was transported, as
if from the tumultuous edge of a hurricane to the still center. A peaceful courage filled me. Soon my breathing began
to ease, and I knew I would be all right.

As long as we are alive, we will experience fear. No
matter how deep our faith, when our life is threatened, or

we think it is, we will feel afraid. But our reaction to fear can change. One time in India I went to see a well-known Advaita Vedanta teacher, Poonja. While in his presence one day, I had a powerful sense of connection to everyone else in the room, and by inference, to everybody in the city, in the country, and on the planet. When I told him about it, he said, "Now you'll never feel fear again." I thought, *Yeah, right. Unlikely!*

Not even fifteen minutes later I was back out on the streets of India as cars, trucks, bicycles, carriages, wagons, people, and animals swirled about the roads in no discernible pattern. Right next to me a pack of dogs went at one another, fighting for scraps of food. Life pressed in too far, too fast—I was afraid all right.

On the one hand, I could have been very disappointed—a scant fifteen minutes of freedom! On the other hand, something was different. I was afraid, but it wasn't the same experience of fear as I usually had. I had a deeper knowledge of the vastness of connection in life, within which fear was arising. I realized that Poonja hadn't meant fear wouldn't come up again in my mind but rather that my relationship to it could transform.

As our faith deepens, the "container" in which fear arises gets bigger. Like a teaspoonful of salt placed in a pond full of fresh water rather than in a narrow glass, if our measure of fear is arising in an open, vast space of heart, we will not shut down around it. We may still recognize it as fear, we may still quake inside, but it will not break our spirit.

MORE AND MORE I've come to know that life will never be served up with guarantees of safety and security. We are not going to stop falling, but we can find faith in the midst of the fall. In his poem "Autumn," rendered here by writer Jonathan Cott, Rainer Maria Rilke describes the bittersweet truth of inevitable change and offers his own statement of faith.

> As from the distance, leaves are falling,
> Fall as if the far-off gardens fade into the sky;
> They fall with gestures of relinquishing.
> And through the night there falls the pressing earth
> Down past the stars in lonesomeness.
> We are all falling. There, this hand falls too,
> Occurring to us all: just look around you.
> Still there is one who holds us tenderly
> As in his hands we fall, fall endlessly.

Through my asthma attack, I came to know that I was being held. I wouldn't use the phrase "in his hands" to describe my own sense of the connection Rilke is talking about, but I see the experience as the same. I feel I was indeed being held by the dharma, a deeper truth, that night. I could never have applied those insights through sheer will or determination. They came to me unbidden, like an act of nature, like a blessing. The understanding had risen up to support me, as though in response to the gift of my heart through all my years of meditation practice.

Experiencing the power of faith doesn't mean we've annihilated fear, or denied it, or overcome it through strenuous effort. It means that when we think we've conquered fear only to be once again overcome by it, we can still go on. It means feeling our fear and still remaining in touch with our heart, so that fear does not define our entire world, all we can see or do or imagine.

As we open to what is actually happening in any given moment, whatever it is or might be, rather than running away from it, we become increasingly aware of our lives as one small part of a vast fabric made of an evanescent, fleeting, shimmering pattern of turnings. Letting go of the futile battle to control, we can find ourselves rewoven into the pattern of wholeness, into the immensity of life, always happening, always here, whether we're aware of it or not.

Being held doesn't halt the falling, doesn't abruptly, according to our desires, change how things actually are. We're not able to stop the unknown from crashing into our expectations, or get the whirlwind of circumstances under

our command. What we can do is let go of the encrusta-
tions of the past and the fearful projections of the future to
connect with the present moment, to find there the natural
flow of life and the myriad possibilities within it.

We can recognize the mystery spreading out before us
and within us all the time. We can step out of the hope/fear
gyration and give our capacity to love a chance to flower.
These possibilities are what hold us. This is where we can
place our faith. Even as we fall, fall endlessly, with faith we
are held as we open to each moment.

CHAPTER 5

despair:
the loss of faith

ALMOST TWENTY YEARS after I first began meditating, I found myself at a retreat being held "down under"
in a convent tucked away in New South Wales, Australia.
The site featured prim gardens, heavy mahogany furnish-
ings, copious amounts of tea, roaming tabby cats, and not
quite enough heat at night. The retreat was under the guid-
ance of Burmese master Sayadaw U Pandita. For the previ-
ous six years, this venerated monk—head of one of the
main monasteries in Southeast Asia—had been among my
primary teachers, inspiring me by both his rigorous disci-
pline and his profound wisdom.

By this time, my life had been intensely changed by my
meditation practice. My mind had been freed of much of
the grief of my childhood. The suffering I'd experienced in
myself and witnessed in others had turned me away from

easy answers and led me to a deeper understanding. I knew what I valued; I had recognized the power of love and compassion. I had an extensive network of supportive friends on the path, and I was intensely satisfied with teaching, which had become my life's work. My life had a wonderful center of gravity because of my spiritual practice, and I felt happier than I had believed possible.

I believed myself ready for what I knew would be a demanding yet liberating retreat. Perhaps reflecting the quaintness of the atmosphere, my inner world felt neatly contained, orderly. Whatever disturbances arose in my thoughts—administrative decisions to be made back home, communications to be smoothed out before any possible misunderstandings grew—seemed vague and distant, issues I could neatly tie up and stow away on a shelf to be dealt with later, at my leisure. However, underneath this casing of peace lay deep pockets of pain held in habitual abeyance, guarded by the thinnest of membranes.

One day in meditation, the membrane tore, and I entered a realm of suffering that would lead me to reach for a new level of faith.

All of us face times in our lives when our pain is so overwhelming that we feel entirely lost in it. It is suffering that forms a seal around us, leaving us no place to go, no remove from which we can safely consider our distress. It is suffering that, in a mockery of alchemy, transposes itself into more of the lead weight of desolation. At times like these, not only do we find nothing to place our hearts upon, we can scarcely find our hearts at all. We feel lost and utterly alone. It's as though we are curled in a dark alleyway while others nearby are in a restaurant enjoying their meals, drinking fine wine, choosing their desserts from among the many selections. If we cry out, no one will hear us. And if they did, they wouldn't care. If by some chance someone cared, we wouldn't deserve it. Our pain is the most enormous thing in the universe, and the most meaningless. The one direction that seems necessary, inescapable, is the night. This is despair.

Doubt is usually considered to be the force that opposes faith. However, in my experience, doubt is an intrinsic part of genuine faith. I think the state of mind that is truly the opposite of faith is despair. Faith is the ability to offer our heart to the truth of what is happening, to see our experience as the embodiment of life's mystery, the present expression of possibility, the conduit connecting us to a bigger reality. When we feel torn away from connection and purpose, we can end up so caught in our state of mind that the whole world seems to exist in reference to our pain.

We may despair because someone disappoints us grievously, or annihilates us casually with their assumptions of who we are, and the world seems void of love. We may despair because someone else is treated so brutally that our sense of humanity is ripped apart. Or we ourselves may have behaved so badly that we cannot imagine ever being redeemed from self-recrimination and regret.

The incline to despair might be gradual—an accumulation of many small experiences—so that we are misled into thinking we are not in danger at all. Then one day we lose our bearings to find we are trapped on a bleak and desolate slope. We long to leave and would, if we could only discover how we got trapped there to begin with.

Or we may be going along in life when suddenly the bottom falls out from under us. We receive a diagnosis of cancer, perhaps, or a loved one dies. This is trauma—an intense, abrupt, and complete alteration of our circumstances—and it can throw us into the depths of despondency.

When we despair, our most visceral torment is that we feel separate from everyone and everything around us, alone and on our own. A woman who lived through the bombing of Hiroshima described her desolation: "When the bomb dropped, we all became completely separate human beings." This is the core aspect of despair—the sense of utter isolation and disconnection. When we believe that our circumstances—inner or outer—will never change, and that there is nothing we can ever do to find love or peace again, our faith is consumed by hopelessness.

It is clear why someone who was in Hiroshima when

the atom bomb fell would experience despair, or those who have suffered in extreme circumstances, such as torture or concentration camps. But some of us feel devastated in situations far less horrendous. Some people live internally as if they are in a war zone, even if they are living in material luxury, sometimes even if they are surrounded by caring family members or friends. If the external conditions of our lives are fairly benign yet we are in pain, we might be ashamed, thinking, *Well, this suffering is so small compared to some. Why should I be in pain?* Viktor Frankl, the psychotherapist who spent years in Auschwitz, understood how the suffering of the Holocaust might be seen as overshadowing any other. In *Man's Search for Meaning,* he wrote that we can never compare the depths of suffering "because suffering is like a gas; it completely fills whatever chamber it is in." When we are in despair, whether with a distinctly impressive cause or not, we feel devastated and alone. Anyone who has ever been in this state of mind, for whatever reason, will recognize the statement "We all became completely separate human beings."

Such suffering seems to be a dead end, senseless, meaningless. Yet in Buddhist teaching, suffering is considered the proximate cause of faith. The phrase "proximate cause" means the most likely or the nearest reason. How could suffering that can destroy a person with its implacability, its remorselessness, be the most likely springboard to faith? Wouldn't it make more sense that positive experiences would lead to faith? Instead, this teaching says that deep suffering, even the night of despair when all faith is gone, can itself be the means to arrive at faith, uncovered, renewed.

My own meeting with despair, in the sweet, pleasant environs of the convent in Australia where I was meditating, forced me to uncover my deepest faith. During one early-morning meditation I was sitting peacefully, watching my breath, feeling sensations move throughout my body, observing the lazy drift of thoughts coming and going in my mind. Suddenly everything abruptly shifted. I had never forgotten the circumstances of how my mother died, but with an immediacy that left no escape, I was engulfed in reliving what had happened that evening when I was nine years old and my mother began hemorrhaging. My heart pounding, my breath catching in my throat, the memory lifted out of the cells of my body, vivid, consuming.

This was more than I could handle sitting in the meditation hall, and I got up and went back to my room. I lay on my bed sweating, too stunned to cry, almost unable to breathe. The swelling of grief that had once closed off my heart drew tightly again. I found myself in a mapless terrain of suffering, a flat, uncontoured land where no change seemed possible. Haunted by my mother's death, I watched the world turn vague and very cold. The despair of feeling completely alone, the anguish and desolation of my childhood once again suffused all time and eradicated all space.

I tried to coach myself out of it. "Well, now you're an adult, and this just isn't like you anymore." I tried to counter my guilt about not saving her with rational arguments. "You were a nine-year-old child, you did the best you could." I tried to manipulate the feelings. "It's not really so bad, shape up." I contemplated fretfully, "Why is this happening to me? I've worked so hard. This is old stuff."

Something was ripping inside me, and I felt disconnected from the person I thought I had become and disconnected from those around me. I had friends at the retreat, but as I thought of them they seemed a bit advantaged and complacent, a little too smug in undertaking their pleasant spiritual pursuits and facing their mild travails. I had a teacher I respected, but as I helplessly watched my connection to him fray, my sense of belonging to a community disintegrated. Dante wrote: "Having left the straight path, I found myself alone in a dark wood." In a culture that tends to deny suffering, I had repeatedly felt alone when I experienced loss or pain. Suffering implied I'd done something wrong, hadn't handled my life right. Here now, at the bottom, I felt completely empty and bereft.

In the middle of this abyss, I remembered I had a

scheduled interview with U Pandita. I opened my eyes and noticed it was almost time to go. Automatically, I pulled on my shoes and set off to see him. Outside the confines of my room, I looked around at the primal, elemental landscape. The sky was a viscous dome of saturated blue. The hard, clear subequatorial sunshine thrust the looming eucalyptus trees and convent buildings into sharp relief. Even the shadows were bold—where there was light there was light, and where there was none the darkness was distinct.

I walked into U Pandita's room, which was much like my own—a cavernous space, with a few pieces of heavy furniture and a threadbare rug. It had seemed picturesque; now it felt devoid of comfort. In accord with Asian custom, I bowed three times and then, sitting down, I hesitantly began to describe my experience to him. Such enveloping pain wasn't what I had anticipated for this retreat, and it wasn't at all what I believed should be happening after years of meditation practice. Embarrassed, I told him I had gone from anguish to a strange kind of constricted numbness. He listened carefully, looked at me calmly, and simply said, "Be mindful of the pain."

What he was suggesting was the essence of what I had been practicing for years. Mindfulness is a specific meditation technique based on being aware of what is happening without clinging to it, pushing it away, or getting confused about its nature (e.g., not thinking that the pain, pleasure, or thoughts will last forever). I absorbed what he said with dispassion, thanked him, bowed, and left.

Still numb, I went off to my room to once again apply this very familiar technique. But I was too disconcerted to use it well. Instead I found my mind manipulating it, with an almost clinical calculation: "If I'm mindful of the pain, I won't feel it as much, and it will go away faster." It was an attempt to bring the suffering to heel, to feel in control, to give conditions a time frame in which to return to what I had expected of the retreat. I wasn't really practicing mindfulness; I was negotiating with my experience to blunt the force of its painful truth.

Over days of suffering, I tried out various tools in a covert effort to make it all go away. I tried to recite the classical refuges, as I had done daily since my first retreat in Bodhgaya: "I take refuge in the Buddha; I take refuge in the dharma; I take refuge in the sangha." For years my heart had been uplifted by holding a vision of the Buddha as an exemplar of what a human being could accomplish, of the dharma as a commitment to the truth, and of the sangha as a reminder of community. Now the recitation seemed hollow, no matter how many times I did it or how much fervor I tried to apply. The fact that I was wielding the recitation as a club to beat back my suffering bypassed my awareness.

I tried the lovingkindness meditation I was so well

versed in, especially offering lovingkindness to myself, but I didn't feel either loving or kind as I repeated, "May I be happy, may I be peaceful, may I be liberated." The lashings of shame, guilt, and anger that tied my heart to inconsolable pain blocked any sense that I might actually deserve to be happy.

All my relentless strategies to make things better or improve the situation failed. Unable to access my faith, I sat doubled over, despair lodged in the pit of my stomach. All I had learned of change, and possibility, and openness was removed, void, unreachable.

My spiritual practice had shown me over and over that withdrawing in fear, disengaging, only compounded the pain. Yet I recoiled from facing my suffering head-on. I was exhausted. I wished I could think of an easier way. I knew I was trying to disconnect from my suffering. To journey through it to repair the brokenness it was revealing was more than I felt capable of handling.

ONE NIGHT I sat up late in the garden. The sky seemed too close, pressing down upon me, filled with stars that looked . . . wrong. The Big Dipper, the constellation I was most familiar with, was nowhere to be found. Instead, here in the Southern Hemisphere, the unfamiliar Southern Cross dominated the night. How would I ever find my way home again? In my early life I'd lost my family; now I'd also lost my footing on the path that had saved my life. I'd lost my comfortable center of gravity in the world. I was on my own, left sitting unhappy and lonely under a too close, alien sky.

A memory of Dipa-Ma arose in my mind. She certainly knew what it was like to have great heartache. Over the course of ten years, two of her three children died, one at birth, one after a few months of life. Her husband, whom she loved very much, had come home from work one day not feeling well and was dead by nightfall. In extreme grief, Dipa-Ma was unable to get out of bed, unable to eat, unable to care for her surviving child. Her doctor came to see her and warned that she might actually die of a broken heart if she didn't do something about the state of her mind. "Go learn how to meditate," he advised.

She was so weak the first time she went to the center that she had to crawl up the temple stairs to begin her meditation practice.

Dipa-Ma's practice enabled her to put the pieces of her experience together in a way that completely altered her life, so that her pain, instead of leaving her stranded in grief, opened her to intense compassion. Deep within herself and even within her suffering she found a power of love that wouldn't diminish, no matter what happened.

When I was preparing to leave India in 1974, I'd gone to see Dipa-Ma to get her blessing. Suddenly, in the midst of our conversation, she said to me, "When you go to America you should teach meditation." I was astonished and immediately protested, "No, I can't do that. I'm not at all qualified." She smiled patiently, as though at a child who has lost the point of a story, and answered, "Yes, you should teach. You really understand suffering. That's why you're qualified to teach." The notion that the unhappiness of my earlier life could serve as the distinction of my abilities seemed most peculiar. She hadn't said, "You have a full grasp of the Buddhist cosmology and all theoretical applications, therefore you should teach." Instead, her criteria were based in the power of moving through great heartache and, rather than being destroyed by it, coming to greater faith—faith in one's self, faith in the power of love, faith in the movement of life itself.

During Dipa-Ma's first visit to the United States, we had sat together under a starry sky as she eagerly sought to spot any differences from the skies of India. Even though her past had left her so bereft by the deaths of her children and husband, she had come out of the tragedy alive and open to life's new experiences. Dipa-Ma had found herself more truly than ever by finding faith and love, even in the crucible of her anguish. Sitting there alone now, under the Southern Cross, I thought if such extreme suffering could serve as the proximate cause of faith, then the suffering of my own despair must also contain a crack of light between shades of darkness. Remembering that the way out of the pain was through it, trembling, I sought the crack. I began to sense a gleam of direction.

Sometimes in the darkness all we can do is keep going, even if the road is rocky, uneven, confusing. A friend once took me to Grace Cathedral in San Francisco to walk the labyrinth. A replica of the medieval pattern set in the floor of Chartres Cathedral in France, the labyrinth is a tool of prayer and contemplation, a spiritual passage. The pattern is a circuitous path to the center and back out again—the way in is also the way out.

I stepped onto the pathway and happily began to follow its twists and turns. I could see that I was very close to the goal—the rosette at the center—when strangely, I found the path taking me back out to the edge again, away from, not toward, the rosette. Puzzled, I stopped, wondering if I had made a mistake. But as there was only the one path to follow, I kept going. After circumambulating the center several times—moving closer, then once again away, then very near the rosette, and back to the edge—all at once I found myself there in the very center. I had attained the goal, not by knowing precisely where I was going, but simply by continuing on.

In Australia, lost in the darkness, I knew the only way home was to follow the path mindfully through the pain. Fearing it, knowing I might many times question whether this path was effectual, still I had to take the chance and keep going. I recalled U Pandita's composure when he suggested, "Be mindful of the pain." He had sat there like a mountain the whole time we were speaking—not a mountain of stony indifference, but strong, dignified, calm. It was not the cultivated poise of cultural mannerism or a clever teaching device, but a soft, steadfast, radiant calm, melded with an abundance of faith that was every bit as soft, steadfast, and radiant. U Pandita had unwavering faith in the process I was going through of moving toward greater awareness, and, most significantly, he had unwavering faith in my ability to go through it.

I recalled a time years before when someone had come to me despondent, feeling completely confined by his unhappiness and unable to look beyond it. Miserable, he said to me, "I've lost my faith." At that time I was the one who sat with unwavering faith in the process. With compassion for his suffering, I responded, "That's okay. I have enough faith for both of us." He immediately looked less forsaken. Now it was my turn to rely on another's faith when the wellspring of my own had dried up.

To be mindful in the way U Pandita was asking meant letting go of my defensive patterns and exposing my vulnerability at a deeper level than I had before. I would have to start with not fighting or resenting the grief, the emptiness I was feeling. Aung San Suu Kyi, leader of the democracy movement in Burma, wrote: "There is darkness in the world, but it is merely an absence of light. All the darkness in the world cannot dispel even the smallest candle flame. We need only to accustom ourselves to the dim vision, and then the blessing of light will grow." Accustoming myself to the dim vision, in the language of mindfulness, didn't mean succumbing to the dimness, but stripping away all layers of pretense so I could actually see what was there.

WHEN WE SEE our pain, whether mental or physical, as a single, solid, monolithic entity, unyielding and oppressive, it is almost impossible to bear. Fighting a consolidated enemy, we feel overcome, helpless, stuck. But when we can be mindful of exactly what is happening, we begin to see that everything we experience is composed of many ever-changing elements. Instead of viewing pain as static and fixed, we begin to see its component parts. Physical pain may be composed of burning, throbbing pressure. Emotional pain such as anger may be made up of fear, hopelessness, frustration. Learning how to work with pain in this way, a musicologist once said, "We would call that 'taking apart the chord.'" When we take apart the chord of our pain, even though the experience may remain difficult, the pain becomes an alive system, with movement and variation and flux. Just as the world is breathing, the pain is

breathing. It's inhaling and exhaling, and there is space between its arisings. Rather than feeling overcome and helpless in the face of a wall of pain, we can find hope, relief in
that rhythm of change.

Over the next few days alone in my retreat room I
rocked back and forth for hours, remembering, and crying.
As I began to explore the ball of suffering in my stomach,
mindfully taking apart the chord, I found notes of fear and
grief and loneliness. I found sadness and resentment and a
tremendous amount of guilt. I also found glimpses of space
between them. As I let in each state, my body became less
rigid, and my armor of despair began to soften. The world
grew a little bigger than my suffering.

For the first time in what felt like weeks, I went outside
for a walk. In the garden, several other meditators were
silently walking. While I knew the particular stories of only
a few people on the retreat, at that moment I knew with
surety that there was pain ribboned through the lives of
everyone I saw there, whether mild unease or severe distress, whether current sadness or potential sorrow.

I had seen suffering aplenty as people revealed their
hearts and lives to me. From my very first months of teaching, when someone came for a meditation interview and
told me about her parents hanging her in the shower and
beating her when she was a child, my career had unfolded
in witness of suffering: physical and sexual abuse, betrayals,

illnesses, depression, loneliness, oppressive relationships, oppressive secrets, exhausting moral dilemmas. Dipa-Ma had been right in telling me that understanding suffering was a good qualification for a life of teaching. And knowing I was not alone in suffering was a good qualification for a life of practice.

As I walked, surrounded by those others on the path, I thought of the story of Kisa Gautami, a contemporary of the Buddha. Like many women of her time in India, Kisa Gautami had been placed into an arranged marriage, but she was not treated well by her in-laws. When she eventually gave birth to a son, her status within the family significantly increased. Not long after, however, her baby died. Kisa Gautami literally went insane with grief. Carrying the body of her dead child, she walked through the streets, asking holy person after holy person to bring her child back to life. Finally she came to the Buddha and begged him to bring her baby back to her.

The Buddha agreed to bring her baby back to life—on one condition: "You must bring me a mustard seed from a house in which there has been no death." And so Kisa Gautami began her search, still carrying with her the body of her child. She went from house to house, asking at each for a mustard seed. As the occupants would turn from their door to fetch a seed in answer to this strange request, Kisa Gautami would say to them, "Wait a minute. Has anyone in your family died? The mustard seed must be from a house in which there has been no death." Each time the response was the same: "That's impossible. Certainly not here." As she went on, hearing the same answer over and over, a change came over Kisa Gautami. She no longer felt so alone and isolated in her grief. She returned home to bury her child, then joined the Buddha to become a nun. It is said that after some time of practice she became fully enlightened.

What is it that brought Kisa Gautami's mind back to balance? What allowed her to move from being nearly destroyed by grief to a place of some composure and peace? Her son did not come back to life; what she ached for had not come to be. Yet what she came to see was that she was not alone in her suffering, that what she experienced was in the nature of things. It's not just a question of "misery loves company." By seeing that everyone, without exception, suffers loss and death, Kisa Gautami joined the whole again. She became part of the natural order rather than feeling separate from it, and this freed her heart to have compassion for herself, and compassion for all beings.

Sometimes when I'm in a great deal of pain, while holding my pain in isolation I secretly build a monument to it, as though I am really very special in my distress. With everything else I've counted on falling away, I find that I try to hold on to that specialness. In my despair I had been doing just that.

Now I remembered that state of connection, so basic and enfolding that it was as implicit as the sun's next rising. And even though I couldn't touch such connection at that moment, I formed a heartfelt wish—to reawaken my realization of that state, to recover faith in a sense of purpose, working to free my mind for the sake of all beings.

A FEW DAYS LATER I went for a walk in the area outside the convent, in what is known as "the bush." Australia is among the oldest, driest, and flattest of all continents, and has one of the most aggressive climates. Yet life abounds there, breaking through impediments, squirming past obstacles, giving rise, again and again, to sustainable forms. Eighty percent of the plants and animals that live in Australia live nowhere else.

The land around the convent was largely sandstone rock, giving the earth a rich golden glow under my feet. The wattles were in bloom, fine hairs like dandelion fluff covering whole bushes in amazing shades of yellow—saffron, cream, flaxen, wheat, amber. The same colors seemed to predominate in the abundant wildflowers as well. I named the hues to myself as I walked in their midst—blond and canary, butterscotch and ocher, lemon and mustard, and a brilliant neon yellow just like a New York City taxicab. It was as though the sun were shining from below me and radiating from all sides.

Surrounded by reflected light, I recalled the words of a discourse U Pandita had given the night before. Quoting the Buddha, he said, "The mind will get filled with qualities like mindfulness or lovingkindness moment by moment—just the way a bucket gets filled with water drop by drop." Looking around me, I could see that the wonder of this field was created by countless small blossoms converging into a vibrant whole. It reassured me that the mindfulness that had been so elusive would build and grow, step by step, into similar vitality and wholeness.

I had wanted my pain to disappear. I didn't want to feel the constriction of fear in my throat, the sadness of a child all alone in the world. But the transformation I was seeking wasn't to be found in what happened to the pain; it would be found in what happened within me in relationship to it. It would be found in opening rather than closing down, in compassion for myself rather than contempt. It would be found in getting reconnected to the wild rush to survive I saw all around me in that golden burst of life. All I could do was deal with whatever experience I was actually facing, and add one more drop to the bucket, one more moment of mindfulness, of transforming my relationship to suffering. Realizing this, I let go of my impatient expectation and

edged out of the despotic reign of time. And kept on practicing.

Faith began to grow, saying that if I opened my heart
and mind big enough to take in the suffering, then there
would be healing—not because the suffering itself is re-
demptive or healing, but because of the opening I was cul-
tivating in the face of it. One of the meanings of "saddha,"
the word for faith in Pali, is hospitality. Faith is about opening up and making room for even the most painful experiences, the ones where we "take apart the chord" of our
suffering to find notes of horror, desolation, and piercing
fear. If I could be willing to make room for my aching
numbness, and the river of grief it covered, allowing it,
even trusting it, I would be acting in faith.

Perhaps this is how suffering leads to faith. In times of
great struggle, when there is nothing else to rely on and
nowhere else to go, maybe it is the return to the moment
that is the act of faith. From that point, openness to possibility can arise, willingness to see what will happen, patience,
endeavor, strength, and courage. Moment by moment, we
can find our way through.

ACCORDING to the Aborigines of Australia, every rock,
every tree, every element of life in their world extends
back to the primordial Dreamtime, where totemic ances-

tors sang themselves and the world into existence. These ancestors, it is said, left a trail of words and musical notes over the lines of their footprints as a map. If you know the song, you can always find your way. On walkabout, Aborigines follow their songlines, the web of notes that marks the earth to guide them.

One night in his discourse, U Pandita mentioned that according to the Buddhist tradition, the sound of the Buddha's voice is still in the world, even though he died 2,500 years ago. That sound, I realized, was my songline. Though I couldn't hear it with my ears, I could hear it with my heart. It voiced the Four Noble Truths, it sang compassion, freedom, the reason for me to be alive. I could hear its resonance again, distant but distinct.

I tried taking the three refuges again and found that if I did the practice without a frenzy of expectation, I wasn't left with an echo of emptiness. Instead of insisting on a finale to my pain as I recited "I take refuge in the Buddha; I take refuge in the dharma; I take refuge in the sangha," I chanted it without a hidden demand, leaving space to hear the chords and notes of my own lineage and mythology and dreams. I remembered the dream of faith.

RILKE WROTE: "So you must not be frightened . . . if a sadness rises up before you larger than any you have ever seen; if a restiveness like light and cloud shadows passes over your hands and over all you do. You must think . . . that life has not forgotten you." For most of us, even in a state of despair it's possible to catch a glimpse into the inclusive nature of life, into the fact that we have not been forgotten, cast aside. Though this might be revealed to us, we might mistrust what we've seen. Sometimes the recognition is as subtle as the release of a sigh; other times it is intense and dramatic, as it would be for me in Australia.

One afternoon I was walking up the staircase to my room, as I had done countless times before, barely noticing now the fraying decor and grubby sconces. I was practicing being mindful of my steps, when all of a sudden I encountered what I can only call a tremendous sense of presence, and with it a feeling of release, joy, and love. I felt like a child thrown up into the air by a tender parent, whose loving arms waited to catch me safely back from my transport of freedom.

I don't know why it was him in particular, but the image of the contemporary Indian saint Maharaji Neem Karoli Baba arose in my mind, as messenger of that primordial love. One of my friends who had met him told me, "He was so vast, no matter how far out I went, he was always there." That's what this presence felt like. I knew with sudden conviction that no matter how deep my despair, life was always there and its essence was this inclusiveness I felt as love; it was big enough to contain whatever sorrow or brokenness might arise. Standing on that staircase, with its shabby wallpaper, worn carpet, and dim lighting, I was rocked by faith in that enormous sense of life.

Compassion arose in me, a tender concern for all of us who, within touching distance of such inclusiveness, usually feel so alone. I found myself spontaneously doing lovingkindness meditation for all beings. Suddenly the image of my mother came into my mind. I realized for the first time that her life and her death were really *her* story, not mine. They were a part of my story, but not the primary part. I prayed for my mother, wherever she was, in whatever life form, to be happy, to be peaceful, to be free from suffering, to be as blessed in that moment as I was, held in the generous embrace of faith.

IS IT NECESSARY to go through despair on a spiritual path, to endure a proverbial dark night of the soul in order to deepen our faith? I don't know the answer to that—but I do know that it is necessary to strip away the entangling, unhealthy ways of relating to ourselves with dislike and diminishment that we are accustomed to. And I know that we need to let go of many things, undergo loss, and unhook from the world's insistence that we cover up our pain in order for us to see what is really important in our lives.

I know that sometimes unbearable suffering is going to be a part of our path because sometimes it is a part of life itself. Such pain burns away superficiality, right down to the marrow of our being. Brought to my knees, my overly defended heart broken open, I learned that suffering could indeed be the proximate cause of faith. I watched as the masks I had used to hide my pain fell, and the boundaries of isolation that kept me from more fully connecting to others and to the wholeness of life crumbled.

Would I have come to a greater faith without that dramatic experience on the staircase? I believe so. I believe every element of my practice had the same end and direction. Seeing my commonality with others, relying on faith in my teacher and on his faith in me, opening to the truth of my experience moment by moment, and seeing the component parts of my suffering were all leading to that same depth of understanding and surrender.

Are all those elements, singly or conjoined, necessarily enough to enable one to emerge from despair with faith? Not always. The path is not the same for everyone. I know that when many people "take apart the chord of their suffering," they find a biochemical component as one of the notes. If depression is a real aspect of one's experience, out of compassion it needs to be addressed as a medical issue. Part of the overall truth we might have to accept is that medication will be the way for the binding filaments of despair to begin to loosen. Perhaps only then will there be enough space for the glimmer of faith to emerge. With the awakening of just that little bit of faith, there can be sufficient energy to keep getting help, to accept support, to begin, or to begin again, walking the path toward liberation.

I know that sometimes things are so bad that no matter what practices we do or what medication we take, we can't seem to generate even that small amount of faith we need for inspiration to keep going. Then, if we can stand inside our pain awhile and wait, over time we may come to also see it as a way into the deepest parts of ourselves and then back out into the world, a vehicle for new insight into who we are and how much we need to care for ourselves and one another. If there is nothing we can do right now but wait, then, as T. S. Eliot wrote, "the faith is in the waiting." If we can but wait, we may yet emerge from despair with the same understanding that Zen master Suzuki Roshi expressed: "Sometimes, just to be alive is enough."

faith in action

IN THE FACE of overwhelming events in the world, we can too easily sink into despair and resignation, considering ourselves small and insignificant, unable to do anything to help. I have found myself on this very slide.

Once when I was traveling with a friend of mine who is African-American, I stood by helpless, watching a painful scene unfold. As she approached a sandwich vendor in the Denver airport to place her order, I saw his face shut tightly against her. The face of my friend grew carefully composed, her voice quieting as she wrapped herself in an aura of invisibility, as though not to jar him. I recalled a story Jan Willis, a professor at Wesleyan University, tells in her book *Dreaming Me,* about the bus journey she took from her home in Alabama to Ithaca, New York, to attend college in the early sixties. During that drive of several days, there was not one single stop where, being African-American, she could sit down and eat at a lunch counter. Forty years later in Denver I stood numb, wondering what progress had been made in trying to redress prejudice if someone had to disappear just to buy a sandwich. What in the world could I do to help create change if all the work done by so many still left us with this?

When I am brought face-to-face with suffering I can do nothing about, I am thrown back years to the mornings when I walked the streets of Springfield, Massachusetts, looking for my father or waiting for a call from the police saying they had found him. During the phase of his treatment when he was placed in less restrictive settings, like halfway houses or nursing homes, he would periodically run away. When we found him, he'd be committed to the hospital again, and we would start the whole process one more time. The cycle went round and round, pretty much until he died.

At times like these, when someone's suffering seems to have no end, when it is too much to bear, we can lose faith in our ability to make any difference at all. But it is exactly at these times when faith is most needed. How do we cultivate a faith that enables us to take positive action in the world against even overwhelming odds? Where can we place our faith that enables us to work to make a difference—especially when it seems that no matter what we do, it's not enough?

When I'm at the ragged edge of an anxious night, when I've tried hard to help someone and am drained by frustration and grief, when the suffering I encounter threatens to pull me down into futility, I need to begin by reminding myself of what I am *not* seeing in the picture of suffering right before me.

For my fortieth birthday, my friend Carol gave me a small picture book. In the center of its vivid red cover were the one-word title—*Zoom*—and the author's name, I. Banyai. Curious, I opened the book and on the first page saw an abstract image of something red and pointy. The next page showed a colorful rooster, whose comb was the image I'd just seen. *This is a book with no words in it, about a rooster,* I mused. *How very peculiar to receive this as a gift when I'm turning forty, not four.* Carol smiled, urging me to go on. I turned the page and saw a picture of children looking through the window of a house at the rooster. *Oh,* I thought, *it's not a book about a rooster; it's about some children who live on a farm.*

As I turned more pages, the children and the house diminished in size until they proved to be pieces in a toy village being arranged by a little girl. *Oh, now I understand,* I thought. *It's a book about a child, and she is the central figure in this story; the other figures were just her toys.*

A page later, the girl playing with the houses turned out to be part of an illustration on the cover of a book being held by a boy. And so on it went. As I turned the pages, I came to conclusion after conclusion about what the book was *really* about. *Okay, now I get it. This is a story about a boy who is on an ocean liner holding a book with a cover picturing a child playing with a miniature village.* But when the entire ocean liner turned out to be part of a billboard posted on the side of a bus, my confidence in my interpretations collapsed.

The bus proved to be part of a scene on a TV screen being watched by a cowboy in a desert, which turned out to be the illustration on a postage stamp, which was on a postcard in the hands of a group of people standing on an island beach. Before I could try to reach another conclusion about the subject of this book, a turn of the page showed the island as seen by a pilot in a small plane. Several pages later, through swirls of clouds, I saw the earth, a jewel-like globe floating in infinite space, then simply a distant white dot. Opened to an immensity of perspective, my vision included every image in an expansive sweep of vision, but was not limited by any one of them. I looked up at Carol and said, "I feel like God!"

There is a far bigger picture to life than what we are facing in any particular moment. To see beyond the one small part in front of us and not think that's all there is, we have to look past our ready conclusions. When we see only the suffering before us and our own actions in response to it, it is no wonder we might conclude that what we do seems inadequate. We may think the final result of something we've done is visible on page four of the story, or page seven. But as we turn page after page, we step outside our own limited perspective and realize that there is more to come. Both the suffering and our efforts to address it are woven into an immense but hidden flow of interaction, a dynamic process of action and consequence that doesn't stop with us and our particular role.

We don't know the ultimate unfolding of any story; certainly not enough to decide that what we do has no effect. When we stand before a chasm of futility, it is first of all faith in this larger perspective that enables us to go on.

This openness of view is also attained by looking more deeply at what is right in front of us. As long as we remain on the surface of life, everyone and everything seems to exist as isolated entities. But when we look below the surface, we see strata upon strata of dynamic interconnectedness. If we look to the greatest depth, Buddhism says, we will see a world where no one and no thing stands apart.

A plate of spaghetti for dinner, for instance, isn't just a jumble of noodles to which we add tomato sauce. Those noodles have emerged out of someone's labor in growing the wheat, their hopes and fears and dreams for their children, the soil and air and rainfall and sunlight that nurtured and supported the growth of that crop. These elements are themselves interactively affected by depletions in the ozone layer and by the loss of the Amazon rain forests, by global warming and by acid rain. A host of environmental degradations, neglectful industries, government regulations, and hopeful interventions are among the conditions giving rise to our plate of spaghetti.

Included in our dinner as well are the efforts of those who shipped the wheat, and those who milled it, and the shopping we ourselves did the night before at our local neighborhood grocery store, kept open by the young proprietor's fearful obsession with a secure old age. Also included is the culinary history of Italy, where pasta became a staple, as well as that of China, where laborers on vast paddies were among the first to eat noodles.

And still this is just a tiny part of the converging conditions. What about the conditions that affected our childhood food cravings, and then our lifelong eating habits? What about the latest board meeting concerning the advertising budget of the company that enticed us to buy their particular brand of pasta? Looking below the surface, we see revealed a world in which a single plate of spaghetti comes out of an entire universe of interconnectedness.

Likewise, our states of mind emerge out of a matrix of conditions. When I sit in meditation and look at the component parts of anger, for instance, I see the strands of fear, sadness, hopelessness. I see guilt over not living up to truths I've experienced about the pain anger causes. I see a silhouette of my mother's early death, leaving me with no role model for an empowered woman. I see an imprint of my mentally ill father, a casualty of nearly everything that went through his mind. I see the struggle of countless people who feel they have no voice, who don't know how to make things better. I see a shameful connection with those who lash out. And I see a thankful kinship with all who, even when they do get angry, try the best they can to live in a way that doesn't cause harm.

I experience a flash of anger as being in *my* mind, squeezing *my* chest, impinging on *my* mood, but seeing it as part of a complex pattern opens me to realizing my inter-dependence with all of life.

What we normally perceive as concrete objects and discrete events emerge from interwoven relationships, our very act of seeing a part of the weave. When we recognize this, rather than feeling locked in by a state of mind, an en-counter, an occurrence, we see that the essential nature of what is happening is not that of a wall, but of a web. When I see only suffering and unfulfilled possibility, I need to re-mind myself of the mystery of life's unfolding—the many linkages that are carrying my efforts through currents of connection to results I may never directly witness.

. . .

IN ORDER TO KNOW the truth of interconnectedness we need to look at the world with what theologian
Howard Thurman calls "quiet eyes." It might be through
silent meditation that we see the hidden patterns of connection that make up our inner life. It might be through
pausing long enough to realize where a plate of spaghetti
comes from. However we do it, softly receiving reality
with quiet eyes rather than pinpointing objects and events
as separate and distinct opens up our view instead of en-
closing it with predetermined boundaries. We take in what
is appearing before reactions and conclusions get fixed.
When we relax into this mode of perception, a different
perspective on reality becomes available to us.

Late one night a friend and I stopped by an art gallery
after a movie. With just twenty minutes before closing, we
were breezing through, looking at whatever seemed most
intriguing. I stopped in front of a poster propped against
the wall, labeled with a sign reading MAGIC EYE. The image
was a reddish-orange blur of color with random patterns.
Looking it over, my friend and I shared several jokes about
the inscrutability of modern art. Suddenly, to my amaze-
ment, a three-dimensional image emerged. It was like
looking into a diorama, with clear and vivid objects at different depths. "Hey, look at the dinosaurs!" I happily ex-

claimed. "What dinosaurs?" my friend retorted. I was mesmerized by the world now revealed in the seemingly random graphic designs. "The ones near the palm trees," I responded, unable to tear my eyes away. My friend called the clerk over, probably to get some help in getting me back to earth. As I continued gazing, absorbed in the magical images, the clerk explained to him that this was in fact a 3-D image, if one knew how to look at it.

The clerk suggested to my friend that he let his eyes relax, to gaze at the space distantly underlying the image. I chimed in, unhelpfully, suggesting he not strain or try to have something special happen. The clerk followed me, recommending my friend look not *at* the picture but *through* it.

After twenty minutes of futile effort, my friend still remained frustrated at his inability to see any cute dinosaurs or a single palm tree emerging from the splotches in the poster. He begged the clerk to keep the gallery open just a few more minutes, and in the end bought the poster, determined to discover how to see what was hidden there.

The apparently random events that make up our lives are like the apparently random patterns in the Magic Eye poster; an underlying set of connections might form a picture that would mean something to us, if only we could see it. When we struggle to see, we end up discouraged and exhausted. When we look with quiet eyes, we begin to see that at the deepest level, everything and everyone is interconnected.

Poet Charles William described this level of interconnection as "separation without separateness, reality without rift." Even aside from a conceptual understanding of this truth, many of us have experienced it in our lives.

For me, a profound sense of non-sensory interconnection occurred when I was involved in a car accident in the late seventies. Some friends and I were on our way out to dinner when a drunk driver, who had fallen asleep at the wheel, collided with us head-on. The rearview mirror tore off and hit me in the face as I was flung out of the passenger seat and into the dashboard. The next thing I knew, I was coming to as people were pulling me from the car and laying me down on the grass. Enveloped by the gray veil of a concussion, I watched as the people around me, the trees, the buildings and cars, began to float, dreamlike.

In the hospital, a nurse asked over and over, "What is your name?" I reached for it but it just wouldn't come. The world, already attenuated, faded even more. As I watched her face change, the random thought that she was worried about me passed through my mind, but I couldn't figure out why she would be.

Lying on the X-ray table, I felt my consciousness leave

my body. I was flying down a tunnel, moving at an incredible speed, thousands of discordant and chaotic images clamoring for my attention. I was terrified. As the intensity and speed accelerated, I grew more and more agitated. Suddenly I heard a gentle voice saying, "Watch your breath."

I had little idea of what anything around me meant, let alone "Watch your breath." I had been practicing meditation for more than eight years by that time, and had watched many a breath, but in the chaos of my mind there was no recollection of anything related to the practice. Yet the voice came again, insistent, "Watch your breath."

Even though I did not have a clue as to why I would do that or how it might help, I struggled to focus on the in-breath and the out-breath. As I breathed, the images began to slow down and the world around me grew more coherent, more compelling than the tunnel. Each time I lost focus and began to "fly out" again, the voice would come back. Each time I watched my breath, I would calm down.

As I was lying there, an image arose in my mind of a friend who was in Burma, living as a monk. I saw him clearly wearing a monk's robe and standing outside an Asian-style building speaking to an older Burmese monk. *That's Alan,* I thought hazily. *Who's he with?* The vision calmed me, and made me feel strangely happy.

I continued to watch my breath, and the vision faded as I felt my consciousness return fully to my body. Slowly I began to recognize the elements of a familiar world. I knew who I was, and that I'd be all right.

Five years later in Massachusetts, I saw Sayadaw U Pandita for the first time. Even though I hadn't seen photographs of him, he somehow looked familiar. In the middle of an afternoon meditation the whole experience came flooding back—the shock of the car crash, the ambulance ride in the night, the tunnel where things moved faster and faster, my terror, watching my breath, and that vision. The older monk in that scene was Sayadaw U Pandita. And Alan had in fact been with him in Burma at the time of the accident.

Some might say that this apparent connection was merely my imagination, a burst of fantasy dictated by my growing regard for U Pandita, and I can't deny that it might have been just that. The story defies logic—but then, so does science these days. Several years later I read about a scientific experiment that provided me with a language that felt linked to my experience.

In the sixties, the physicist John Stewart Bell theorized that particles that were once connected will, when separated, behave as if still connected, regardless of the distance between them. Some years later a French physicist, Alain Aspect, conducted experiments offering physical proof of Bell's theorem. In Aspect's setup, which used lasers to excite calcium atoms, a single photon was passed through a special crystal that split it into two "daughter" photons. The two daughter photons were allowed to travel off in opposite directions. Each was randomly directed to one of two devices that determined the direction of its polarization or "spin." Aspect's results showed that no matter how far apart the photons were, when the spin of one was measured, its partner simultaneously showed the opposite, or complementary, spin. The correlation was instantaneous: It happened faster than the speed of light.

Theoretically, according to Aspect, the distance of the whole universe can separate these two particles, and when one spins "up," the other spins "down." If one spins "right" the other will spin "left." The inescapable conclusion is that two particles that were once connected will continue to behave in relationship to each other, even when separated by vast stretches of time and limitless space. Einstein called this kind of thing "Spooky" action at a distance.

To me this characteristic of elementary particles seems connected to the spooky experience I had of Sayadaw U Pandita while lying on the X-ray table. It is as though we had been spinning through lifetimes, apart yet related, and in a critical moment our link had been made conscious again. According to the Buddhist cosmology, we have all died and been reborn countless times, in the course of which we have been one another's mothers and children and students and teachers and friends and enemies. We varied events of our lives, whether desired or untoward, are contingent, related, in concert.

This interdependence is both good news and bad news. The bad news is exemplified in environmental devastation. Mismanagement, recklessness, or cruel disregard in one area can affect air quality, flooding, migratory patterns, and biodiversity across regions and continents around the world. Scientists have traced ecological patterns revealing that widespread deforestation of Tibet under fifty years of Communist Chinese rule has led to soil erosion in the high Himalayas, which in turn has resulted in devastating floods in China, India, and Bangladesh, and has disrupted weather patterns across Asia. Some experts even hold that Tibetan deforestation has affected weather throughout the entire Northern Hemisphere.

The good news is that, according to the same law of interconnectedness, what we do individually and collectively *does* make a difference. The essence of chaos theory is something called "sensitive dependence on initial conditions." This means that a very small perturbation or change in a system can have a profound effect; that tiny, local actions can have widespread, far-off, complex consequences. This idea, discovered by the meteorologist Edward Lorenz, has come to be known as the Butterfly Effect, after a talk Lorenz gave at the American Association for the Advancement of Science titled "Predictability: Does the Flap of a Butterfly's have loved one another and hurt one another, laughed together endlessly, and cried an infinite number of tears in one another's arms. And we have reminded one another to breathe.

Either viewed through the dharma or through science, the fundamental condition of reality is wholeness, interrelatedness. This immense, interlinked, commonly hidden world is the realm where our actions play out. Knowing we are intimately connected to this bigger reality upholds our faith as we take action in the world.

THE LATE Wilfred Cantwell Smith, a scholar of comparative religion at Harvard, described faith as "an orientation of the personality, to oneself, to one's neighbor, to the universe; a total response, a capacity to live at more than a mundane level; to see, to feel, to act in terms of, a transcendent dimension." The vast universe of responsiveness is that "transcendent dimension." When we live and act within that reality, we begin to understand how we can have faith in our actions.

The reality that everything is connected doesn't imply that the events in life are predetermined, or "meant to be," as though we need to feel ground down by the inexorable conditions of life. Rather it evokes a picture of our lives as seen from a perspective in which we and others and the

Wings in Brazil Set Off a Tornado in Texas?" In truth our actions spread out through a vast web of links, continually bearing fruit, whether we are aware of it or not. And sometimes we do get a glimpse of this.

The course U Pandita was teaching when I first met him was a three-month retreat. He gave unusually extensive talks, translated by a superb interpreter. Later, several friends and I decided to put out a book based on the course. We raised money for the transcription and found an interested publisher. I asked a friend who is a writer, Kate Wheeler, to turn what was basically an oral transmission of classical Asian Buddhism into a manuscript that would honor that tradition while also engaging the Western mind. She did a wonderful job, and the book, titled *In This Very Life,* was published.

At the time of publication, I thought, *Well, we've done something good, something that honored our teacher and that will be of some small service. It's not going to be a best-seller, but it does express a certain teaching through very clear language, and it's really an excellent vehicle for the limited impact it will have.* I more or less put it in the minor-good-deed category in my mind. Several years later I radically reassessed my evaluation when I learned of the impact that small "local action" had in a far-off place.

Aung San Suu Kyi, leader of the pro-democracy movement in Burma, has long been one of my heroes. Her country, where many of my meditation teachers are from or have studied, is ruled by a brutal military dictatorship, and Suu Kyi has dedicated her life to protesting their policies. In 1989 she was placed under house arrest for her political activities. Her sons were sixteen and twelve at the time, and she would not see them or her husband for many years. Refusing to accept anything from the military, she didn't even have enough money for food at times. She became so weak that at one point her hair fell out and she couldn't get out of bed.

During the six years that she was under that phase of house arrest, the military offered her many opportunities to leave Burma, but it was clear that if she left she would not be allowed back in. By staying, she knew she would continue to be a symbol of hope for democracy for the people of Burma. She chose to remain, which won her the Nobel Peace Prize, awarded to her while she was still imprisoned.

For a brief period the military released Suu Kyi before confining her again, and she was able to speak and write about her experience. In discussing her spiritual life, Suu Kyi wrote: "The spiritual dimension becomes particularly important in a struggle in which deeply held convictions and strength of mind are the chief weapons against armed repression." She related how her attempts at meditation had foundered due to a lack of instruction. She would sit on her bed, gritting her teeth, trying to practice, but would only become tenser. And then her husband sent her a book that changed everything. That book was U Pandita's *In This Very Life*. Through it she had learned how to meditate, and it became her main source of spiritual support during those intensely difficult years.

I was stunned when I heard that story. A Burmese teacher had come to Barre, Massachusetts, we created this book, and somehow it ended up back in Burma in the hands of a woman I admired immensely and would have given anything to help, if I'd only had an inkling as to how. Whenever I hear someone minimize the value of their good works, I think of how without designing it, a small group of friends ended up helping to relieve suffering in a way beyond what we could have imagined.

We can never know how our actions will ripple out and affect others. We may, through force of habit, disparage ourselves, considering an action to be inadequate, or resign ourselves to its certain mediocrity, but we can't possibly know the ultimate result of anything we do. T. S. Eliot wrote: "For us there is only the trying. The rest is not our business."

Yet when we assess the value of our actions, we often do so in terms of whether or not they will produce a certain consequence—doing the good we envisioned, in the time frame we anticipated. If it doesn't work out that way, we may lose faith in what we do and grow dispirited. Unless we can guarantee the response we want, we might even decide not to take certain actions at all. Such attachment to achieving results can lead to relentless expectation, burnout, and the desolating habit of feeling we can never do enough.

In Buddhist teaching, however, the immediate result of an action, and how others respond to it, is only a small part of its value. There are two other significant aspects: the intention giving rise to an action and the skillfulness with which we perform it. The intention is our basic motivation, or the inner urge that sparks the action. The skillfulness with which we act involves carrying out the intention with sensitivity to and awareness of what might be appropriate in any given situation. While the skillfulness of an action has a great deal to do with the result, it is the intention behind an action that is critically important. We can't control the response to an action. We can do our best to act skillfully, but it is at the level of intention where we make a crucial choice. An action can be motivated by love—or by hatred and revenge. Self-interest can be the source of what we do—or generosity can be. If our intention is wholesome, we can have faith in the workings of interconnectedness to continuously unfold our action, no matter how small or big, in positive ways.

Whenever I teach lovingkindness retreats in an urban

setting, I ask the students to do their walking meditation out on the streets. I suggest they choose individuals they see and, with care and awareness, wish them well by silently repeating the phrases of the practice, "May you be happy, may you be peaceful." I tell them that even if they don't *feel* loving, the power of their intention to offer love is not diminished. One retreat took place a few blocks from downtown Oakland, California. Since we were directly across the street from the Amtrak station, several people chose to do their practice on the train platform.

When a train pulled in, one woman from the class noticed a man disembark and decided to make him the recipient of her lovingkindness meditation. Silently she began reciting the phrases for him. Almost immediately she began judging herself: *I must not be doing it right because I feel so distant. I don't have a great wash of warm feeling coming over me.* Nonetheless, reaffirming her intention to look on all beings with kindness instead of estrangement, she continued, reciting, "May you be happy, may you be peaceful." Taking another look at the man, who was dressed in a suit and tie and seemed nervous, she began judging him: *He looks so rigid and uptight.* Judging herself, she thought, *Here I am trying to send lovingkindness to someone and instead I'm disparaging him.* Still, she continued repeating the phrases, aligning her energy with her deep intention: to be a force of love in the world.

At that moment the man walked over to her and said, "I've never done anything like this before in my life, but I'd like to ask you to pray for me. I am about to face a very difficult situation in my life. You somehow seem to have a really loving heart, and I'd just like to know that you're praying for me."

Life can't be explained by a perfectly linear predictability: "I thought this, so he felt that." It is a lot messier, and more outrageous, and more mysterious. However, this remarkable "coincidence" can still illustrate the point: Even though the woman didn't perform a concrete physical or verbal action, her commitment to positive intention apparently had an effect. When our intention is to do good for others, and we nurture that intention, we can have faith that in some way, often unknown to us, it ripples out.

Several recent scientific studies have explored the power of prayer and distant healing. The preliminary findings are startling. Even when people are unaware of such efforts on their behalf, it appears that these interventions have an effect. For example, in a study at California Pacific Medical Center in San Francisco, AIDS patients who, without their knowledge, were prayed for had significantly fewer new AIDS-related diseases, less severe illness, fewer doctor visits, and fewer and shorter hospitalizations than patients in the control group who were not prayed for by those in the study.

A research project undertaken at a fertility clinic in Korea showed even more amazing results. Women trying to conceive who were prayed for at a distance became pregnant at twice the rate of those who received no prayers. I was amused that the author of the report and his colleagues apparently had to consider whether or not to publish their findings, since they seemed so improbable. In the end, they decided that the difference in the pregnancy rates between the two groups of women was too significant to ignore. Chancing ridicule, the researchers went ahead and made the results public. Whenever I read studies such as these, I think of those who offer prayers of lovingkindness for the well-being and happiness of all who live, prayers which, for all of us, may be quietly interlaced throughout the breadth of our joy.

Even when we don't know what to do to make things better for someone, or when whatever we do seems likely to be of little consequence, we can have faith that we are not isolated individuals in a fragmented world. We can have faith that the power of intention links our actions to a vast web of interconnection.

ONE MORNING during a visit to California, I was sitting on the beach in Santa Monica, idly looking at the Pacific Ocean. My mind released into the expanse of water and into glistening swirls of imagination. I saw pirates who had sailed this same ocean, ships laden with treasure, leaving turmoil in their wake. I saw explorers setting out with daring and conviction and a thirst for unbounded seeking. I saw navigators drawing on their skills at witnessing and learning to step beyond the commonplace rhythms of local village life. As I sat there enraptured, I could imagine myself as any of these adventurers, and felt within me the power of reaching beyond restriction, of bravely venturing forth, of fearing nothing. I felt I could do anything.

Then I noticed that someone had come to sit down beside me. I turned and looked into the face of a young woman. By her clothing and demeanor I could see she was one of the urban homeless. Her eyes were dead, hopeless, offering nothing, expressing nothing, puncturing my dreams of bottomless courage with their bottomless suffering. I felt ill at ease, stricken by my own powerlessness, not knowing what to say. I felt I could do nothing to make things better, to take away her suffering.

One of the most brilliant and best-known teaching metaphors in Mahayana Buddhism is that of Indra's Net. Indra, in ancient Vedic cosmology, is the lord of the firmament; his net is the universe, a net of infinite proportions. At every node where the strings of the net meet, there is a glittering, highly polished jewel. Each jewel reflects every other jewel in the net; to look at one jewel is to see them all, as in a hologram. As the Avatamsaka Sutra, an important Buddhist text, describes it, "The process of reflection is infinite." In this view, to really see another person is to see ourselves, and to see ourselves is to see all beings.

When we know how intertwined our lives are, we know that the life of a homeless woman on the beach has something to do with our own. We can't avert our eyes, looking around those who suffer, or through them, for a more pleasing vista. Our picture of life necessarily includes them. Rather than regarding the suffering of others as a threat to our closely held happiness, we know that turning away from them is like turning away from ourselves. In this way, we recognize community in a wider and deeper reach.

Seeing the truth of our profound interconnectedness opens us to an unstudied altruism that is simply a reflection of a more honest life. Trusting that we are fundamentally linked strips away the armor of difference and separation. I turned and faced the emptiness in the homeless woman's eyes, dropping my temptation to recoil in the face of her condition and my own sense of helplessness. I smiled at her, silently recited, "May you be happy, may you be peaceful," and sat with her awhile, sharing an ocean view with its castings of infinite possibility and change. I didn't give her money, though I often have given in such situations in the past. I didn't decide to go advocate for better shelters or increased care for the mentally ill, though on other occasions that might have been the correct thing to do. I sat with her and recognized her as a human being, a fellow wayfarer, in the larger sense a part of me, rather than an alien creature.

It is in the nature of our existence that we can't, by decree, or effort of will, or fervent desire, or even by all-consuming love, make the pain go away for someone. We can't, no matter how hard we try, always get someone who is resistant to accept help, or bring a frightened person to safety, or successfully demand change in an intractable institution. Many times our efforts will be foreshadowed by defeat even as we try to create change. And many times our hearts will break when we do in fact fail.

But if that inevitable sorrow is joined with faith in interconnectedness, rather than bitterness at the nature of things, we can more likely get up the next morning and once again do the best we can, knowing that in this interconnected reality, even the smallest action done with good intention is consequential.

What others have done before is impacting reality as we experience it right now. What any of us do right now has an effect over the reaches of time and space. Even when we feel helpless, we can find support in this truth. We can, with love and compassion, continue to offer our hearts beyond the hurdle of pain, stirred by faith to act the best we can in the life we all share together.

We may not comprehend why there is so much suffering in this world, why some people behave so badly toward others, but we can count on hatred never ceasing by more hatred, but only by love. We can't predict how our actions will turn out, but whatever we do will have impact and consequences. There is no knowing what the future holds, or what lies on the horizon, but no matter what happens, the lives we live each day are part of a greater whole. We can place our faith on these certainties.

CHAPTER 7

abiding faith:
faith in ourselves

FROM HER ISLAND in the New York City harbor, the Statue of Liberty has welcomed countless immigrants, including my grandparents, at the end of their wearisome journey and the beginning of their life in a new land. Her welcome of all, even those unwanted by anyone else anywhere, is professed in the moving inscription at her base, written by the poet Emma Lazarus:

> *Give me your tired, your poor,*
> *Your huddled masses yearning to breathe free,*
> *The wretched refuse of your teeming shore,*
> *Send these, the homeless, tempest-tost to me:*
> *I lift my lamp beside the golden door.*

I've adored the Statue of Liberty for a long time and admit to having bought many photos and souvenir replicas of

150

her from shops in New York City. As a woman bearing light, as a symbol of bottomless compassion, she has long been my personal icon. In Hinduism, the personal deity to which one offers one's heart is called an *ishta dev*. The ishta dev is chosen from the vast pantheon of gods and goddesses for the qualities one most wants to emulate. If I were to adopt an ishta dev, it would be Lady Liberty.

As an image of inspiration, she seems as enduring as the freedom she symbolizes. Like the Great Pyramid or the Mahabodhi stupa in Bodhgaya, I can't imagine her not being there. Yet even monuments that have endured for centuries can crumble in an instant. Between the second and fifth centuries A.D., monks painstakingly carved two massive Buddhas, standing about 120 feet and 175 feet tall, out of a sandstone cliff in the area of Afghanistan. Even though I hadn't yet seen them on my various trips to the East, I loved knowing they were there. They felt like guardians of peace, so tall they could silently watch over me and the whole restive world. In March 2001, despite vigorous efforts on the part of the world community, the Taliban of Afghanistan blew them up. Monuments to eternity, reduced to charred rubble by tanks, shells, and rockets.

The Statue of Liberty might herself one day be reduced to a memory, like the twin towers that once stood nearby. In the days following the attack on the World Trade Center in September 2001, I feared for her. Then a new image of her appeared on newsstands and in souvenir shops—an image that is profoundly related to faith. She stands, lamp aloft, promising freedom to the tired and wretched, while huge plumes of black smoke billow up from behind her. Beneath that smoke, in the rubble and ruin of the World Trade Center, lay terrible tragedy. Yet despite the horror and destruction, she still stands there in welcome. As my ishta dev, she reminds me that, even in the midst of devastation, something within us always points the way to freedom.

Anything outside of us that we look to for inspiration can crumble into dust. No symbol, no construction, no condition, no relationship, no life is immune to change. No beloved and esteemed teacher, no friend or loved one can avoid dying. Devastated by the deaths of her husband and children, my teacher Dipa-Ma remembered asking herself, "What can I take with me when I die? I looked around me: My dowry—my silk saris and gold jewelry—I knew I couldn't take them with me. My daughter, my only child, I couldn't take her. So what could I take?" At that moment she decided, "Let me go to the meditation center. Maybe I can find something there I can take with me when I die." What Dipa-Ma found formed the core of what she could have faith in, something that couldn't be torn away from her through change. What can any of us place our faith in that endures? According to Buddhist teachings, to discover that is to know the deepest level of faith.

The offering of one's heart happens in stages, with shadings of hesitation and bursts of freedom. Faith evolves from the first intoxicating blush of bright faith to a faith that is verified through our doubting, questioning, and sincere effort to see the truth for ourselves. Bright faith steeps us in a sense of possibility; verified faith confirms our ability to make that possibility real. Then, as we come to deeply know the underlying truths of who we are and what our lives are about, abiding faith, or unwavering faith as it is traditionally called, arises.

Abiding faith does not depend on borrowed concepts. Rather, it is the magnetic force of a bone-deep, lived understanding, one that draws us to realize our ideals, walk our talk, and act in accord with what we know to be true. Theologian Paul Tillich defines this kind of faith as alignment with our "ultimate concern," those values to which we are most devoted, which form the core of what we care passionately about. An ultimate concern is not an interest that is merely a fashion or a whim, but one that is a centering point for our lives.

When we wake up in the morning and picture the dealings of our day as consequential, we tell ourselves a story that is based on our ultimate concern. We remind ourselves of loving our neighbor or remembering God. When at the end of our day we recall its events and arrange them in a pattern that reveals something significant, our ultimate concern is what we reference in the arranging. Because of abiding faith in an ultimate concern, the day wasn't just a series of flashing moments, lost to us now and amounting to nothing. We count on our ultimate concern not just for ballast when things get rocky, or for a sense of easy comfort on a bad day; we count on it for light.

Our ultimate concern is the touchstone we turn to over and over again, the thread that we reach for to convey a sense of meaning in our lives. It is the glue that connects the disparate pieces, the frame that gives shape to the picture of our experiences. We turn to our ultimate concern when afraid, or bewildered, or when we don't quite know who we are anymore. We turn urgently toward our ultimate concern to give us context when we are shaken by loss or the threat of loss; we turn there quietly when something we wanted disappoints us or begins to fade away.

For many, a principle such as justice serves as an ultimate concern. Bernice Johnson Reagan, a singer with Sweet Honey in the Rock, was a dedicated civil rights activist in the early sixties. Recalling the danger she and her friends faced in challenging segregation in Georgia, she says, "Now I sit back and look at some of the things we did, and I say, 'What in the world came over us?' But death had nothing to do with what we were doing. If somebody shot us, we would be dead. And when people died, we cried and we went to funerals. And we went and did the next thing the next day, because it was really beyond life and death. It was really like sometimes you know what you're supposed to be doing. And when you know what you're supposed to be doing, it's somebody else's job to kill you." Unwavering faith in justice enabled these civil rights workers to carry on through the tremendous ups and downs of their lives.

We might have abiding faith in the lawfulness of nature—seeds regenerating after a fire, rivers flowing toward the sea, renewal following decay. After the atom bomb fell on Hiroshima, it is reported that a wave of panic swept through the city when rumors spread that grass, trees, and flowers would never grow there again. Had the disaster been of such proportions that the laws of nature had exploded with the bomb? As we know, even in the face of massive human intervention, the grass and trees and flowers did grow again in Hiroshima. Several people, describing their experience of that time, say that it was only once they learned that natural law was still intact that they had the faith to go on.

An aspiration, too, can be the ultimate concern in which we rest our abiding faith. In *Zen Mind, Beginner's Mind,* Suzuki Roshi writes: "Even if the sun were to rise in the west, the bodhisattva has only one way." That "one way" of a bodhisattva is the commitment to compassion, to dedicating the activities of one's life to the benefit of all beings. We might know success or failure, great wealth or barely enough to get by, acclaim or a quiet life, but we can be inspired by our sense of purpose in all these circumstances.

For those who aspire to the freedom from suffering taught by the Buddha, the primary repository of abiding faith is our own buddha nature. Because Buddhist teachings arise out of the experience of a human being, rather than being conferred by a deity, great emphasis is placed on abiding faith in oneself, in one's true capacities.

Lack of faith in our own potential limits our sense of possibility to habitual concepts. It keeps us from sensing who we might yet become, or how we needlessly circumscribe our lives. Whatever we might be conditioned to believe, the teachings say that beneath our small, constricted, Lucy-defined identity lies the innate capacity for awareness and love that is buddha nature. This is what faith in ourselves rests upon.

The texts liken buddha nature before it is awakened to "flowers before their petals have opened, a kernel of wheat that has not yet had its husk removed, a store of treasure hidden beneath an impoverished household." That potential for love and awareness we can place our hearts upon is present regardless of our particular conditioning or background or traumas or fears—it is not destroyed, no matter what we have gone through or what we will go through. Although some people are completely out of touch with that

FAITH

capacity—they can't find it, or don't trust it—it is always there.

What distinguishes faith in ourselves from conceit is the fact that conceit lays claim to specialness, while our fundamental nature is not personal—it's universal, it's shared. When we look at the Buddha or a great teacher, we can see our own potential for happiness, for vibrant wisdom and sustained compassion—a potential that all beings share. However, if we stop at faith in another, admiring him or her and overlooking ourselves, our faith remains incomplete.

ALTHOUGH I'D SEEN IT in all my earlier teachers, abiding faith came most alive for me through my teacher Khenpo. He tirelessly pointed the way for me to unfold this same quality of faith in myself. By the time I met him, I had been practicing meditation for years. I knew without question that all things pass, that attachment is the cause of suffering, that my refuge lay in my own buddha nature, in the dharma, in the sangha. I had developed faith in these truths and faith in my ability to realize them. But Khenpo was such a bright light that some of my old tendencies arose. At times I simply wanted to merge with him as a way to hold on to the intensity of his beauty. Being close to him sometimes seemed more important than getting closer to myself through practice. As much as he pointed the way to faith in my own buddha nature, it would only be through losing him that my faith would profoundly mature.

I first met Khenpo in Paris in 1991. An old friend, Surya Das, an American trained as a Tibetan Buddhist lama, was eager to introduce us. He ushered me into a room painted an overwhelming brilliant yellow-orange, where Khenpo was meeting with a group of French schoolchildren. I had half-expected to find a stately pedagogue surrounded by awkward and awestruck students. Instead the room was alive and vibrant, Khenpo laughing, teasing, and playing with the children. The moment I saw him a constriction in my heart eased, one that I hadn't even realized was there. He looked up at me, and as soon as our eyes met I felt I'd come home. The light I sensed coming out of him was brighter than even the extravagant color of the walls surrounding us.

Khenpo was the most spacious person I'd ever met. It seemed as though the wind passed right through him and translucency was the major component in his makeup. Many times in his company I had the strange sense that we were standing in a wide-open field, great empty expanses spreading out in all directions. Even if we were in a crowded little room, the walls closing us in seemed to evaporate. Perhaps this effect was a reflection of Khenpo's wide-open consciousness and huge unbounded heart. Being with Khenpo was the closest I'd come to experiencing transformation through just being in the presence of a realized person. Yet he was entirely unself-conscious, like a magician unattached to his own magic.

Whenever I had the chance to watch Khenpo do his daily *puja*—ritual practice—I was struck by his devotion and the intensity of his faith. Bowing to the Buddha, his face brimmed with joy, as if he were welcoming his best friend home. The puja had a festive air, as if he and the Buddha were celebrating a bounty of faith together: Khenpo's faith that following the path of the Buddha could lead to freedom; the Buddha's faith in every person's potential to be free. Khenpo's faith wasn't blind or self-satisfied; it was simply based on the unwavering knowledge of his own experience. His treasure truly was within, and his confidence in that was the foundation of his abiding faith.

I loved Khenpo as much as I have ever loved anyone in my life. He was my teacher, the man from whom nothing in me was hidden, and my attachment to him was strong. I once had a dream in which someone asked me, "Why do we love people?" I answered, "Because they recognize us." I think this is true. When someone recognizes a basic goodness within us, beyond our habits and conditioning, when someone recognizes who we fundamentally are, it is the most important thing that can happen to us, and we respond with great love. Khenpo recognized and encouraged the innermost nature of all his students, and we loved him deeply.

However, the more powerfully and consistently he directed me to unfold my own capacities, to have faith in my own true nature, the more I relied upon his presence to point me there. When I complained about feeling inadequate, Khenpo challenged me with: "Why is your sense of aspiration so small, so anemic? Why not aspire to be a liberated being, for the sake of all beings? Why not?" And I would think, *Isn't he a great being to say such a thing?* When I felt obsessed with what a friend might be thinking of me, Khenpo would remind me again, "The thoughts that arise in someone else's mind are also empty. They're insubstantial and impermanent. Why let them define you?" And I would think, *He's right. That's such a liberated view.* When I brandished a meditation experience like a badge of achievement, Khenpo directed me back to the truth: "The price of gold goes up and down, but the value of gold remains the same. Your experiences will always change, will go up and down, but what is of innate value in you lies in your awareness and love." And I would think, *Khenpo's buddha nature is so obvious, his qualities of awareness and love so well developed. How fortunate I am to be near him.*

The extent to which I was dependent on Khenpo's presence to sustain faith in my self was sharply revealed one spring day in 1999 with a sudden phone call. I was celebrating a friend's birthday when the news arrived that Khenpo had a brain tumor and was probably dying. Every light in the room seemed to suddenly dim. Feeling as if I were about to step back into the airless chamber, the compressed and lonely world of a bereft child, I found myself thinking, *His death will be the worst thing that has ever happened to me.* As soon as I could, I made arrangements to travel to France to see him.

In the days before leaving I often looked at the pictures of Khenpo and the dove on my mantelpiece. I wondered if Khenpo was relating to the flying away of his life as he had to the flying away of the dove. I wondered if I would be able to relate to his death with any kind of similar grace.

KHENPO WAS STAYING in the Dordogne region of southwestern France, on the grounds of a Tibetan retreat center. Joseph Goldstein and I landed in Bordeaux, then drove there, past majestic old oak and chestnut forests, and through villages with stone huts, churches, abbeys, and castles dating as far back as the thirteenth and fourteenth centuries. Dordogne is well known for its rich human history, beginning with the cave paintings and petroglyphs of Lascaux and Les Eyzies-de-Tayac, some 200,000 years old. It was a trip through layers of time, with eras twisting and blending until the present moment seemed laden with all that had gone before.

We pulled up at Khenpo's house at dusk, the horizons bathed in a wash of rosy light. I was apprehensive, not sure what I would find, or what I should say, or how I should be. Khenpo's wife, Damcho, greeted us with a hug and brought us inside. Khenpo was sitting in a wheelchair in the living room, looking at the trees through a sliding glass door framed with pots of red and violet flowers. I was shocked at his appearance—his face was swollen from the brain tumor, giving him a curiously fetal look, as if he were closer to birth than to death. When he saw us he seemed to regroup, smiling and giving us each a thumbs-up. He greeted Joseph warmly and, displaying his uncanny ability to read my thoughts, told me I was doing well, my meditation practice better than when he had last seen me (which was true). I stood there, acutely aware of how much I didn't want to lose him, and of the futility of that wish.

The days soon settled into a routine: sitting with Khenpo while he sat quietly with us, or while his attendant fed and washed him. Damcho's sister cooked Tibetan food, which we all shared. Sometimes Khenpo's doctor would visit and give us reports on his condition. Everyone there took turns wheeling Khenpo around in the living room, while we chanted sacred mantras. The day when it was first my turn, I was nervous, worried about doing it right, worried I might somehow tip over the wheelchair and hurt him, maybe even kill him. It was as if all my anxiety about Khenpo's impending death was projected onto this terrifying tour around the living room.

As I pushed the wheelchair, Khenpo felt my growing unease. Finally he sighed and said, "Go sit on the couch and meditate," and called Joseph over to replace me. While Khenpo had unwavering faith in my buddha nature, he quite correctly wasn't too sure about my physical coordination. I was delighted to go sit down, but as I went to meditate I wondered if he knew just how afraid I was at the thought of his death.

Those next few days at Khenpo's house were like resting in the arms of unconditional love. The air was filled with a sense of blessing. Damcho took care of Khenpo and each of us with undiminished radiance and generosity. People who had studied with Khenpo came to pay their respects and express their gratitude. A young monk from Bhutan often stayed up all night with Khenpo, and seemed delighted to do so. One night Joseph and I watched as Tulku Pema, eminent teacher and director of the retreat center, got on his knees to feed Khenpo. Tulku Pema looked absolutely blissful. I whispered to Joseph, "Look at his face. He looks like he's feeding the Buddha."

I was astonished—and deeply inspired—as I watched the quality of the love in those around Khenpo. Even though they were sad to see him dying, they loved him freely and completely. They weren't loving him out of duty for what he had given them. They weren't withholding love because he could no longer provide them with wise and brilliant lectures or make them laugh. They didn't want anything from him.

The quality of love each of them was displaying was a reflection of the very buddha nature Khenpo had invariably seen in them. This buddha nature, with its two wings of love and awareness, is what we had invariably seen in Khenpo. Despite his condition, he would pull himself back from whatever faraway place his mind had gone to in order to express delight in the mantras chanted around him, to kindly greet people, to reveal beautiful visions he had had of deities offering teachings. Even though he was preparing to die, he would reach outside himself to ask me how I was feeling, to whisper a meditation instruction, to smile at me or give me a thumbs-up. His energy poured over me, and I could feel his undeviating confidence in me seeping into my pores, trying to tell me I'd be all right, reminding me of the power of my own unconditional love.

164

In 1971, sitting under the bodhi tree in Bodhgaya, I had resolved to develop the love of a buddha. A buddha loves—like Khenpo with the dove, like Khenpo letting go of his life—beholding change, while remaining openhearted and caring. This quality of love, which manifests as devotion, compassion, and lovingkindness, is not based on maintaining things as they are, or on fearfully trying to prolong what we like. Because of this, it remains undiminished throughout the inevitable changes of life.

The preeminent force in conventional love, whether in intimate relationships, work partnerships, or families, is attachment. Attachment is always dependent on conditions being a certain way. We love someone or something as long as we are pleased, as long as there is no change in our satisfaction. Once our pleasure is threatened, the love is threatened. Attached, we relate with tremendous fear to the inevitability of change. This is what I went through when Ram Dass had his stroke.

Being there with Khenpo, I found myself moving between love and attachment. Despite my resolve to develop the love of a buddha, I was holding on to Khenpo, my heart pleading for him to remain in that body, as my teacher, in this lifetime, without ever going away.

The other facet of buddha nature, which was so evident in Khenpo, is awareness. Like unconditional love, awareness is based in nonattachment. It is the faculty of directly seeing what is happening, without the intrusion of bias, without holding onto or pushing away any experience.

A student approached Khenpo one evening during a retreat and asked how to get better experiences in meditation, and more of them. Khenpo laughed. Holding out his prayer beads, he said, "That kind of desire is like taking this mala and stretching it and stretching it to make it bigger and better, until it finally breaks. What's important is not the particular experience we're having, which will change anyway; what's important is confidence in the nature of awareness itself."

One of the best depictions of awareness comes from Chogyam Trungpa Rinpoche. In a class he was teaching he drew a loose V shape in the center of a large white sheet of paper. "What is this a picture of?" he asked. The students all responded, "It's a bird." "No," Trungpa Rinpoche said. "It's a picture of the sky, with a bird flying through it." Like the sky, awareness is open and spacious. If we focus on this spaciousness rather than on any particular thought or feeling arising in it, we are free.

There are so many birds that fly through the sky of our awareness—myriad thoughts and feelings like lilting nightingales, drumming woodpeckers, chattering parrots, elegant herons, imposing hawks, and the vultures that seem to be circling some days, tempted by our exposed and wounded hearts. But if we become entranced by any of them, we forget the sky. None of the birds will give us free-dom—each will take us off to its own particular realm of endless change. Each will tempt us to adopt its identity and forget the vast spaciousness of our buddha nature.

We can place our faith in this awareness because no matter what passing thought or feeling arises, the nature of awareness remains unchanged—pure, open, unimpeded. There is a story adapted from the Buddha's teachings that points to this unchanging nature. If someone standing in a room throws paint around, it is sure to damage the walls, floor, ceiling. Awareness is like a room with no limiting di-mensions. No matter how much "paint" is thrown around, there is no disfiguring impact, no place for it to land.

The open nature of awareness can bear anything with-out becoming damaged. Relying on this unsullied nature, we can see whatever happens to us as part of the rising and passing of all phenomena. This understanding doesn't make us passive, but gives us the ability to see things with a dif-ferent perspective—knowing that there is always an intact place within us. Then we needn't be paralyzed by our suf-fering. Watching Khenpo so close to death, I saw the qual-ity of his awareness—he was responsive to everything without being defined by any one experience, not even the one of his dying. I knew I had to approach my life as he approached his death—finding refuge in that same power of awareness.

At the end of our visit, Khenpo was lying in bed, too weak to get up. As we meditated next to him, I prayed fruitlessly for time to stop. Then it was time to go. Khenpo gathered his breath to give us a last bit of advice for our practice, encouraging us to trust absolutely the nature of love and awareness. I knew that no matter how much I would miss him, Khenpo's departure would force me to have faith in my own buddha nature rather than relying only on his. He thanked us for coming to see him, and placed his trembling hand on Joseph's head, then mine, to give us a blessing. As I walked out, I realized that of all the many deaths and losses in my life, this was the first time I'd been able to say good-bye to someone I loved.

LESS THAN TWO MONTHS after I saw him in France, Khenpo died. A few days later, I entered a retreat led by a brilliant young Tibetan teacher, Tsoknyi Rinpoche, who had studied extensively with Khenpo. In the early days of that retreat, I could see him quietly taking on more and more of Khenpo's wisdom, as if he were absorbing him. It reminded me of passing through Dordogne, en route to Khenpo's house, with layers of time melding into the present moment.

Though heartened by this new sense of what lineage means, I still felt deep sadness as I thought of never seeing Khenpo again. I realized that rather than asking, as Dipa-Ma had, "What can I take with me when I die?" I had reversed the question and wondered what he would be leaving behind with *me* when *he* died. I had gone to France half-hoping Khenpo would give me something of himself that would perpetually support me—a talisman, a pithy saying, anything I could cling to after he was gone. He had left me only with myself, and it didn't seem to be enough.

One beautiful afternoon I was outside doing walking meditation. The blue sky was without a cloud. Another person came up to me, and though we were in silence, she pointed up the road toward the crest of a hill and whispered, "Have you seen the rainbow?" It was a clear day. How could there be a rainbow without any rain? Feeling almost pushed, I ran frantically up the road.

In Tibetan Buddhism, the fact that the rainbow exists—a vivid array of many colors, yet insubstantial, born of light—has made it a symbol of the true nature of life. To see one is considered auspicious, an indication of blessings from Buddhas, bodhisattvas, teachers, or deities.

I arrived at the top of the hill, and sure enough, the arc of a huge rainbow, beautiful, translucent, vibrant, stretched across the sky. I felt as though it were emanating from Khenpo's heart. My own heart, so recently aching, was suddenly filled with joy. My body was so light it seemed I could fly. I felt as close to Khenpo as I ever had when he was alive. Delivered through that closeness was a riveting level of understanding truths that I'd known, but with a new intensity and conviction: Just as I couldn't hold on to that rainbow, trying to hold on to people, to objects, to appearances, everything transient in life, would only bring more suffering. No matter what happens, we can place our faith in the deepest part of ourselves, our buddha nature. I could almost hear his voice reminding me, "Your experiences will always change, will go up and down, but what is of innate value in you lies in your love and awareness."

There is a popular Tibetan story about a powerful bandit in India who, after countless successful raids, realized the terrible suffering he had been causing. Yearning for a way to atone for what he had done, he visited a famous master. "I am a sinner," he declared, "and I am in torment. What is the way out? What can I do?" The master looked the bandit up and down then asked him what he was good at. "Nothing," replied the bandit. "Nothing?" exclaimed the master. "You must be good at something."

The bandit was silent for a while, then said, "Actually, there is one thing I have a talent for, and that is stealing." The master was pleased. "Good," he said, "that's exactly the skill you need now. Go to a quiet place and rob all your perceptions, then steal all the stars and planets in the sky, and dissolve them in the belly of emptiness, the all-encompassing space of the nature of mind."

"Emptiness" is the Buddhist term for the insubstantiality of our experiences as they arise and pass away. Standing at the top of the hill, I could begin to recognize the truth about my attachment to Khenpo. I knew that he would tell me, like the teacher in the story, that its nature was unsubstantial and like all experiences it would pass away. I knew that, like the thief in the story, if I'm good at sadness and regret, if I'm good at anxiety, then I can use those things for greater understanding. If I'm good at self-doubt, thinking, *I'm not going to say this right,* or *I should be handling this better,* then this doubt, too, can be seen like any painful state, as a bird flying through the sky of awareness. With faith in the power of awareness, I would be able to see my whole tangle of turbulent, painful emotions for what they were— changing, moving, evanescent. They didn't have to lead me into greater hopelessness or anger or fear. I could be aware of them without getting caught by them. Instead of locating myself in the grief or the sadness or the regret, I could locate myself in awareness of them.

Even though Khenpo was gone, I could turn to the deepest part of myself to discover the strengths I'd need each day to take the possibility of freedom and make it real.

Rather than losing love as I lost him, the love and awareness he'd awakened in me were *in* me, a part of me, and therefore could abide far past the span of his life.

Faith in our buddha nature won't crumble in adversity, won't insist on rainbows fixing their position in the sky, won't mistake the ungovernable elements of life for the underlying truths on which we can rely. Like the Buddha reaching down to touch the earth while sitting under the bodhi tree, unwavering faith knows to call upon the trustworthy earth of our own nature. This is what we can reach for to bear witness to our struggles—knowing that it is constant, reflects a deeper truth, is unmarred by the drama being played out on the surface. This is where we discover the most essential, enduring elements of our lives—the truths about ourselves that join us to all others, the truths that echo throughout time, the truths that free us from dependence on the roiling world. The buddha nature within us is what makes abiding faith in ourselves authentic, not a pipe dream or aimless fantasy. It is because we all have buddha nature that the Buddha's story of life can become our own.

Our passion, our joy, our calm, and our confidence are all rooted in this offering of our hearts to an expanded vision of who we truly are and the love and awareness we are capable of. With this understanding, we don't have to approach our suffering as though cut off from love and the pulsing of life. We can remember that suffering doesn't have to close us down and lead us into despair, as though stranded in a world where goodness is for others and others exist at a remove from us. Holding this vision of who we truly are, we can keep Lucy from weaving together the threads of our life story. Holding this vision, we can emerge from whatever suffering we encounter, not broken and embittered, but with an ever-replenishing wellspring of unwavering faith.

epilogue

To offer our hearts in faith means recognizing
that our hearts are worth something, that we ourselves, in
our deepest and truest nature, are of value. When we live
from this knowing, our offering is complete, generous,
bountiful. I find this unstinting faith perfectly expressed in
one of the verses of Lal Ded, or Lalla, a fourteenth-century
mystic from Kashmir. Lalla says:

> *At the end of a crazy-moon night*
> *the love of God rose.*
> *I said, "It's me, Lalla."*

As if renewing her acquaintance with an old friend,
Lalla addresses her God casually, sweetly, intimately. En-
chanted, I feel inspired by her winsome response, her calm

expectation of being remembered. "Hi, you remember me, don't you?" Lalla offers herself completely, no reticence due to feeling a lack of self-worth, no questioning of her absolute right to be there, face-to-face with the vastness of her ultimate truth. Without any doubt, the heart she brings is worthy. For a long time after I discovered this poem, it was my touchstone. I wanted to be like Lalla, close up to the truth of life.

One day, faced with an urgent turning point in my life, that favorite line arose in my mind, transformed into a phrase that launched me from admiration of Lalla to standing in her place. It was no longer "It's me, Lalla," but "It's me, Sharon." It's me, Sharon, right up against the question of what it means to be alive, and having to someday die. It's me, Sharon, part of a constantly changing reality, with all surety falling away. It's me, Sharon, not even one slight step removed from my own potential for love and awareness and my ability to realize them. It's me, Sharon, no longer appreciating from a distance Lalla's up-front, textured, vibrant connection to her truth, but directly face-to-face with my own.

Like Lalla, we all have that absolute right to reach out, without holding back, toward what we care about more than anything. Whether we describe the recipient as God, or a profound sense of indestructible love, or the dream of a kinder world, it is in the act of offering our hearts in faith that something in us transforms, and what may have been merely a remote abstraction flames into life. "It's me, Lalla," becomes "It's me . . . whoever we are," proclaiming that we no longer stand on the sidelines but are leaping directly into the center of our lives, our truth, our full potential. No one can take that leap for us; and no one has to. This is our journey of faith.